Urban Rage In Bronzeville

Social Commentary In The Poetry of Gwendolyn Brooks, 1945–1960

B. J. Bolden

Third World Press Chicago

Printed in the United States of America

05 04 03 02 5 4 3 2

Cover design by Taahira Mumford

Library of Congress Cataloging-in-Publication Data

Bolden, B. J. (Barbara Jean), 1946-
Urban rage in Bronzeville: social commentary in the poetry of Gwendolyn Brooks. 1945–1960/ by B. J. Bolden.
p. cm.
Includes bibliographical references and index.
ISBN 0-88378-194-8 (cloth:alk. paper)
ISBN 0-88378-195-6 (pbk:alk. paper)
1. Brooks, Gwendolyn, 1917—Political and social views. 2. Literature and society—United States—History—20th century. 3. City and town life in literature. 4. Social problems in literature. 5. Afro-Americans in literature. 6. Anger in literature. I. Title.

PS3503.R7244Z58 1999
811'.54—dc21 97-30831
CIP

Third World Press
7822 S. Dobson
Chicago, Il 60619

CONTENTS

TO GWENDOLYN BROOKS

Your stately stroll toward me
        kindles a flame of poetic fire.
Your coal blackness and wine blood
        increase your strength
        and inordinate beauty.
Your laughter hides historical pain.

You are life celebrated!

You are the mother of Blackness
        and Ethnicity and Majesty.
You share your power with the earth;
We must learn the strength of your love.
Your affection is the base for our being.

You have known suffering and sacrifice
        and oppression and strength.
An African King shares his need for you
        from afar.
Your Blackness must permeate the Universe.

YOU ARE!

Leonard A. Slade, Jr.

Acknowledgments

I am grateful for the scholarly assistance of Emily Stipes Watts, George Hendrick, Alice Deck, and Haki R. Madhubuti for their readings, critical assessments, and valuable suggestions on this manuscript. I also extend my appreciation to the following individuals for their contributions to my work: Michael Flug and Robert Miller of the Vivian G. Harsh Research Collection of Afro-American History and Literature at the Carter G. Woodson Regional Library, Chicago, Illinois; Tred Merrill at the Chicago State University Library; Vera Mitchell and Rosemary Stevens at the African-American and Africana Library at the University of Illinois-Urbana; Keith Appler, Judd and Dabney Bankert, Richard and Mildred Barksdale, Margaret and Betty Bolden, and Carol Severins. I offer sincere thanks to Talmadge Milan for his encouragement of my work and his technical assistance in the completion of this project. Asante Sana to Gwendolyn Mitchell for her calm demeanor and astute attention to detail.

Grateful acknowledgment is made for permission to reprint "To Gwendolyn Brooks" copyright ©1988 by Leonard Slade, Jr., which first appeared in *Another Black Voice: A Different Drummer.* Reprinted with permission of author.

A Critical Context

In her first autobiography, *Report from Part One* (*RPO*), Gwendolyn Brooks asserts: "I am a writer perhaps *because* I am not a talker! It has always been hard for me to say exactly what I mean in speech. But if I have a written clumsiness, I may erase it" (141). Ironically, Brooks is often referred to as "quiet" "reserved," and "shy" in demeanor, ironic perhaps, because those terms suggest a reticence or hesitancy with words.[1] She even referred to herself in those terms: "I was naive, I was shy, and a very sweet girl," prior to her awakening to the reality of her own cultural identity as a Black woman (175). But the force of her poetic utterances need not be heard in myriad decibels of verbal sound, nor in the rage of an angry countenance, since the persistence of protest is evidenced by her words. In the preface of *RPO* writer Haki R. Madhubuti (Don L. Lee) aptly describes Brooks: "a quiet force cutting through the real dirt with new and energetic words of uncompromising richness that are to many people unexpected, but welcomed by millions" (3).

Over fifty years of literary publications, accompanied by Brooks' prestigious stature as Poet Laureate of Illinois, since 1968, attest to her prominence and acceptance as an artist. However, the universal appeal of Brooks often masks the ironic acclaim which has hovered over her career like a cloud-laden sky. She has been assailed by the proprietary attitudes and persistence of both Black and white communities who, having honored her with accolades and awards, deem themselves to be the target audience of her pointed social messages, expressed through her poetry and prose. And though recognized for her early attention to women's issues, simultaneously, she has been criticized for not defining herself as a feminist. But underneath a cool and calm exterior, Brooks' real spirit erupts in a volcanic-like profusion of words, symbols, and syncopated rhythms that ultimately defines her target audience as Black, urban, oppressed survivors.

Like many critics, Madhubuti sees a dramatic change in Brooks' pre-1967 and post-1967 works. The catalyst for that change was the 1967 second Black Writers' Conference at Fisk University, Nashville, Tennessee. For the first time, Brooks came into contact with a younger generation of writers and encountered the rage of the 1960s, which was a symbolic assertion of the need for Black writers to address their Blackness in their artistic works and direct those works to a Black audience.[2] The militant utterances of Amiri Baraka (LeRoi Jones), John O. Killens, and Hoyt W. Fuller fell on Brooks' receptive ears, and she responded thoughtfully and enthusiastically.

In her autobiography, she writes: "Until 1967 my own blackness did not confront me with shrill spelling of itself. I knew that I was what most people were calling 'a Negro'; I called myself that, although always the word fell awkwardly on a poet's ear;..." (83). Further, Brooks expresses her dramatic reaction to the young, fiery poets in her self-analysis:

> I—who have 'gone the gamut' from an almost angry rejection of my dark skin by some of my brainwashed brothers and sisters to a surprised queenhood in the new black sun—am qualified to enter at least the kindergarten of a new consciousness now. New consciousness and trudge-toward progress. I have hopes for myself.(86)

Following the Fisk conference, Brooks expressed a desire to redirect her work to her own community in a newish voice of poetic clarity that would invite the masses of people to comprehend her social messages. As she states, "My aim in my next future, is to write poems that will somehow successfully 'call' all black people . . ." (*RPO* 183). She left the conference understanding that "the black emphasis must be, not *against white,* but FOR black" (45). This 1967 awakening of her new Black consciousness acted as the impetus for a visible change in the themes, tone, form, and execution of her poetry.

Brooks' pre-1967 poetry exhibits a focus on craftsmanship that is indicative of the concentration on form, symbolism, and compression evident in much of the Modernist poetry of the 1940s.[3] Her deft handling of the intricacies of traditional European prosodic techniques is visible in her use of conventional stanzaic forms, including couplets, terza rima, quatrains, and Chaucer's seven-line rime-royal, especially in her second book, *Annie Allen.* Brooks' versatility is also discernible in her agile use of free verse, blank verse, ballads, Shakespearean and Petrarchan sonnets, and sonnet variations. Like the noted white writers of the day, T.S. Eliot, Ezra Pound, and William Carlos Williams, whose poetic styles were greatly admired by the American public, Brooks too proved herself so technically proficient in poetic form that her literary peers acknowledged her brilliant technical skill by awarding her the Pulitzer Prize for *Annie Allen* in 1950.

Unfortunately, the question of whether or not Brooks' proliferation of stylistic devices obscures her early social messages to her own cultural community is mired in a matrix of the charges leveled against her poetry of the 1940s.[4] The ensuing complexities, created by her use of conventional forms, obscurantism with language, and perplexing compression, have stymied scholarly examinations of her early work, rather than created a dynamic emergence of theoretical perspectives that could enlarge the telescopic lens for explicating her work. The challenge in reading Brooks' poetry is to explicate it with a cultural and historical specificity that recognizes her expertise in the skillful execution of prosodic devices and classic rhetorical techniques, while at the same time freeing her poetry from the interpretative grips of pure formalism to expand the reading of it in recognition of her incisive social commentary regarding the economic, political, and social climates in America that affect all Americans, and especially her own cultural community.

The reality of Gwendolyn Brooks is that she is, and always has been, a "citizen poet" who uses the daily activities of the Black, urban population of Bronzeville to depict the many facets of their American reality.[5] By creating vignettes that characterize the lives of everyday people in her urban ghetto, Brooks dramatizes the microcosm of Black life in America by creating a poetic portraiture of the afflictions caused by their poverty-ridden and racially divisive living conditions and an astute portrayal of their stoic responses. In her first book of poetry, *A Street in Bronzeville* (1945), Brooks sketches a blueprint of the urban ghetto of Bronzeville to highlight the day-to-day impoverished living conditions Blacks face and how they survive the rigors of second-class citizenship, expressed in economic deprivation, underemployment, tenement housing, and inferior military status. Both the oppression and the vitality of the community are especially vivid in the major poem of the work, "The Sundays of Satin-Legs Smith." A complex portrait of Satin-Legs is painted that situates him amid dire poverty while gracing him with the flair of a "dandy" who flaunts his meager finery. Brooks then captures a global perspective that begins with a penetrating scrutiny of the American military at home, in the poem "Negro Hero," and culminates with a critical glimpse at the troops abroad in the "Gay Chaps At The Bar" sonnet series.

The apex of Brooks' second work, *Annie Allen* (1949), is "The Anniad," a mock-epic that converges around the bildungsroman tale of a young, Black, urban girl and makes a pointed social commentary on the dire problems of intraracial color conflicts and the adherence to white standards of beauty that haunt the Black community. Finally, in *The Bean Eaters*

(1960), Brooks' commentary on the ills that sabotage the American ideals is clear and emphatic. She targets events which were the harbingers of the Civil Rights Movement and highlights the extent to which racial segregation, social inequality, and rampant discrimination still threaten the American creed of "freedom and justice for all." The central poem of the work, "A Bronzeville Mother Loiters in Mississippi. Meanwhile, a Mississippi Mother Burns Bacon," addresses the 1955 lynching of a Chicago youth, Emmett Till, who was murdered for allegedly flirting with a white woman in Money, Mississippi.

Although *The Bean Eaters* is generally read as a work of social commentary, *A Street in Bronzeville* and *Annie Allen* are more often read from the tenets of formalism which, ultimately, render an inadequate focus on the political, social, and economic implications of these earlier works. Because early profiles of Brooks depict her as a "quiet" and "shy" poet, her subtle injections of social commentary often fall on deaf ears, while her easily visible and extensive knowledge of poetic technique is highly touted and rewarded. Even though Brooks has consistently resisted the overt title of a "protest" poet, she has ardently defended the explicit rage in her work which emanates from her attention to the social climate in America.

Editor George Stavros once asked her whether *The Bean Eaters* was "more socially aware" than her previous works, since some critics had noted its attention to race, class, and gender issues.[6] Brooks' response was terse: "when I am ready to write I write as urgently and directly as I possibly can...And I am not writing poems with the *idea* that they are to become 'social forces'" (author's emphasis *RPO* 151, 153). And in response to interviewer Paul Angle's query, "Is the poet affected by today's social unrest?," Brooks writes:

> The poet, first and foremost an individual with a personal vision, is also a member of society. What affects society affects a poet. So I, starting out, *usually* in the grip of a high

> and private suffusion, may find by the time I have arrived at a last line that there is quite some public clamor in my product. (Brooks' emphasis *RPO* 138)

Conversely, among those who have opted not to see Brooks in the full range of her avowed political perspective is Keneth Kinnamon, who, basing his conclusions upon her first autobiography, labels her one of many African American women who is more interested in the theme of "community" than in "individual rebellion."[7] The reality is that Brooks has been a staunch public rebel since she decided to publish her first book of poems, defining the "Black Belt" as the foundation of Black economic impoverishment. Where Kinnamon is correct, however, is that the sense of community is a vital force in Brooks' life and that quite often her expressions of "individual rebellion" are a force for institution building in the community. As an expression of that rebellion, albeit for cultural unity, Brooks formulated a radical redefinition of herself from "Negro" to "Black," during the volatile period of protest for much younger writers in the 1960s. Then, after over twenty years of publishing with Harper and Row, Brooks, at the age of fifty, opted to support the efforts of smaller Black publishing houses. Additionally, Brooks abruptly and publicly altered her stance on integration, notwithstanding her substantial white readership. And finally, Brooks created poetry unencumbered by traditional stylistic devices so that her pointed social message would be accessible to a larger contingency of her own cultural community.

In a 1983 interview with Claudia Tate, Brooks argues for the social content evident throughout her canon of poetry. Acknowledging the fact that in her pre-1967 work, she "wasn't writing consciously with the idea that blacks *must address* blacks, *must write* about blacks," she still insists that "much of that early work was addressed to blacks, but it happened without my conscious intention" (author's emphasis Tate 40).

Brooks insists that her poems in *A Street in Bronzeville* and *Annie Allen* are "politically aware" and asserts: "I believe it takes a little patience to sit down and find out that in 1945 I was saying what many of the young folks said in the sixties. But it's crowded back into language like [that of *Annie Allen*]" (42). Brooks' most explicit statement in the interview is clear: "My works express rage and focus on rage" (Tate 43).

Viewing Brooks' poetry from this vantage point supports a reading of her entire canon as one which is socially significant from her earliest works. As a serious and conscientious artist with a perceptive and avowed social consciousness, Brooks must be viewed in the entirety of her life and work, surrounded by the crucial elements which serve to mold the poet who sees her life and her art in uncompromising terms. Indeed, her work *is* rage-filled. Her poetry is the sight of unfulfilled Black people who inhabit *A Street in Bronzeville*, searching for a road map to the American Dream, in spite of evidence to the contrary. Her poetry is the sound emitted by the unfulfilled when their rage is at its zenith, a sound that Brooks translates into a palatable sophistication in *Annie Allen*. Her poetry is the sense of rage underlying all the poetic decorum wielded by an expert poetic quill that still defines those who strive to become full Americans, yet who are consistently rejected in *The Bean Eaters*. Indeed, this is the rage of Bronzeville, and this is the rage of Gwendolyn Brooks.[8]

Gwendolyn Brooks
A Biographical Sketch

Gwendolyn Brooks has been Poet Laureate of Illinois since 1968, when she succeeded Carl Sandburg, the first Poet Laureate of Illinois. Though she has been nearly a lifelong resident of Chicago, Brooks was actually born in Topeka, Kansas, June 7, 1917, and arrived in Chicago shortly after birth. She attended public schools on Chicago's South Side, graduated from Forrestville Elementary School, Englewood High School, 1934, and Wilson Junior College, 1936. She is the daughter of the late David and Keziah (Wims) Brooks. In 1939, she married the late Henry Lowington Blakely II, author of *Windy Place*. She is the mother of two children, Henry L. Blakely III, a California software designer and Nora Brooks Blakely, founder and director of Chocolate Chips Theater in Chicago.

Brooks is a nationally recognized poet, teacher, and lecturer who has earned over seventy honorary degrees from colleges and universities across the country. She has taught at the University of Wisconsin-Madison, City College of New York, Columbia College of Chicago, Northeastern Illinois University, Elmhurst College, and Chicago State University. Some of the special honors accorded Brooks in the state of Illinois include the Gwendolyn Brooks Center for Black Literature and Creative Writing at Chicago State University, the Gwendolyn Brooks Junior High School in Harvey, the Gwendolyn Brooks Cultural Center on the campus of Western Illinois University in Macomb, the Edward Jenner School Auditorium in Chicago's Cabrini Green community, and the engraving of her name on the Illinois State Library in Springfield.

Brooks was awarded the Pulitzer Prize in 1950, for her second book of poetry, *Annie Allen* (1949), and has continued to receive national recognition and awards. In 1985, she became the 29th Consultant in Poetry to the Library of Congress. She is a member of the American Academy and Institute of Arts and Letters. Her awards include: the American Academy of Arts and Letters Award, the Shelley Memorial Award, the Ainsfield-Wolf Award, the Kuumba Liberation Award, two Guggenheim Fellowships, the Frost Medal from the Poetry Society of America, a National Book Award nomination for *In the Mecca,* and the National Endowment for the Arts Lifetime Achievement Award in 1989. A special honor bestowed upon Brooks is being the only American to receive the Society for Literature Award, University of Thessaloniki, Athens, Greece, 1990. She is a Jefferson Lecturer, 1994, and National Book Awards Medalist for Distinguished Contribution to American Letters, 1994. She is the sixth recipient of the *Sewanee Review's* Aiken-Taylor Award. In October 1995, she received the National Medal of Arts at the White House; and in October 1998, she was inducted into the National Literary Hall of Fame for Writers of African Descent by Chicago State University. Brooks has published many books of poetry, both for adults and children, a novel, *Maud Martha,* 1953, writing manuals, and two autobiographies: *Report from Part One,* 1972, and *Report from Part Two,* 1996.

Chapter I

A Historical Perspective: Gwendolyn Brooks, the Chicago Renaissance, and Bronzeville

Gwendolyn Brooks' literary training commenced when she began to understand that her youthful journal musings were more than childish notes and daydreams. Brooks' parents recognized her unique talents early on and played a major role in nurturing her identity as a writer.

In *RPO*, she recalls that her father was a man who "revered books and education" and provided the budding writer with an old desk "with many little compartments" (56). At the age of "four or five," her mother permitted her to tag along for the rehearsals in expressive recitations geared for the older children at the Carter Temple Church on Chicago's South Side (49). Brooks also wrote the plays performed at the church by the ten-to-thirteen-year-old youngsters. Thus by the time she was eleven years old, Brooks was a self-declared poet, compiling her "Careful rhymes. Lofty meditations" in her notebooks (55). And by the age of seventeen, Brooks was striving to confirm her mother's pronouncement that she would be the "lady Paul Laurence Dunbar" (56). In her unpublished manuscript *Songs After Sunset* (1935–1936), bound with blue construction paper and tied with red yarn, the young poet offers her own whimsical views of life and love as she gropes for poetic maturity.[1] Within nine years, she would publish her first book of poetry and within fourteen years, she would win the Pulitzer Prize for her poetic efforts.

However, there is a second and little-known phase of Brooks' literary education that also contributed to the poetic expertise she has exhibited throughout her literary canon. As Brooks was striving for poetic maturity in the 1930s and 40s, Chicago was in the heyday of a literary renaissance of Black writers who would ultimately celebrate the talents of their peers like Richard Wright, an early "revolutionary" poet; Margaret Walker, best known for her first collection of poetry, *For My People*, which won the Yale Younger Poets Award of 1942; and Gwendolyn Brooks, who received early literary claim for her first two books, *A Street in Bronzeville* (1945) and *Annie Allen* (1949), for which she earned the Pulitzer Prize in 1950.[2]

Although literary historians and critics readily acknowledge New York's earlier Harlem Renaissance of Black writers and artists from 1920 to 1935 and give credence to the later literary outpouring of the Black Arts Movement, which occurred adjacent to its political sibling, the Black Power Movement of the 1960s, little recognition has been bestowed upon the Chicago Renaissance of Black writers and artists who livened up Chicago's literary scene from 1935 to 1950.[3]

The climate of the 1930s that fueled the Chicago Renaissance was born of two events: the migration of thousands of Southern Black agricultural workers, mostly sharecroppers, to Chicago in search of better economic conditions and the 1929 stock market crash that created the 1930s economic catastrophe, the Great Depression. Prior to the 1930s, Chicago's Black population was miniscule, approximately 2% of the city's total population in 1910, 4.1% in 1920, and up to 6.9% by 1930. Between 1850 and 1890, over one-half of Chicago's ethnic make-up was foreign-born; after 1890, Chicago's one million plus population included second generation Irish, Germans, and Scandinavians, who, by 1910, were joined by Poles, Jews, Italians, Russians, Hungarians, and Greeks. On the heels of these early immigrants, over 60,000 Southern Blacks arrived in Chicago to fill the employment gap left by whites fighting in World War I. Factory jobs at good wages lured these Black Southerners to the steel mills and packing houses of Chicago's South Side. By 1930, the stream of Southern Blacks, who began migrating north between 1916 and 1919, had swelled to such proportions that what had started out as a small "Black Belt" on Chicago's South Side quickly became a "Black Metropolis" and grew into one of the largest concentrations of Black people in the world. Thus, the demographic base for Chicago's literary renaissance of Black writers was born and appropriately named "Bronzeville."[4]

The literary climate of Bronzeville had added impetus from several sources throughout the Chicago Renaissance. First, in October 1933, a Black Chicago librarian, Vivian Gordon Harsh, the first Black librarian to head the George Cleveland Hall Branch Library on Chicago's South Side, created an intellectual environment, known as the "Book Review and Lecture Forum," where Black writers could meet and share their literary works-in-progress, while being privy to the discussions of some of America's most recognized Black writers.[5] By the late 1930s, and for the next 20 years, Harsh would attract an impressive array of featured speakers, including writers Langston Hughes, Zora Neale Hurston, Alain Locke, Arna Bontemps, Richard Wright, William Attaway, Margaret Walker, Gwendolyn Brooks, and social scientists, St. Clair Drake and Horace Cayton.

With Harsh's encouragement, the Works Progress Administration's (WPA) Federal Writers' Project, under President Roosevelt's New Deal, added economic stability to the informal gathering of Black writers when they authorized a study called "The Negro in Illinois," from 1936 to 1942. Both Horace Cayton (1936–1939) and Arna Bontemps (1939–1942) served as directors of the project. In the financially tumultuous times of the 1930s, most of the aspiring writers welcomed the employment provided by the Illinois Writer's Project and enthusiastically embraced the opportunity to contribute research and writing to the study, pursue their own creative projects, and simultaneously help Harsh to build her "Special Negro Collection" of literature and history.[6]

A second impetus to the Chicago Renaissance was established in May 1936, when Richard Wright created a literary space for Chicago's Black intelligentsia. He had long pondered a means by which he could counter the isolation of the Black writer, create an ongoing intellectual forum to exchange theoretical concepts, and initiate an environment for peer-review of literary works-in-progress, much like Harsh's legacy of the Book Review and Lecture Forum. Wright initiated his plan at the 1935 launching of the National Negro Congress when he organized and took the helm of the South Side Writers' Group, which was later led by Margaret Walker. The group met regularly at the Abraham Lincoln Center on Oakwood Boulevard for about two years. The South Side Writer's Group, as it came to be known, was composed of similarly aspiring artists, poets, novelists, and dramatists, who met regularly to discuss their topics and works in Black history, literature, and current events.

Upon his arrival in Chicago, in 1927, Wright initially held a series of low-paying, menial jobs: at various points, he was a delivery boy for a Jewish delicatessen, dishwasher for a cafeteria, street sweeper, ditch digger, and postal worker. But it was not until his considerable writing talents convinced WPA officials in Chicago that he would be a strong asset that he was appointed to the Illinois Writers' Project in 1935.

Although Wright hailed from Natchez, Mississippi, he was often referred to as the "greatest of Illinois writers," based upon the literary canon he produced during the Chicago Renaissance, initially as a proletarian poet. In part, Wright's acclaim grew because he took a revolutionary stand in the late 1930s when he positioned himself as a writer for the cause of the class struggle in America and a supporter for the "Communist belief that art is a weapon" and should be used in a frank and propagandistic manner.[7] As such, he brought a new social interpretation to Negro fiction with his novel of Black life in Chicago's ghetto, *Native Son* (1941), an earlier novel, fictionalizing his experiences as a Chicago mail sorter, *Lawd*

Today, written in 1935 but published posthumously in 1963, and his first collection of novellas, *Uncle Tom's Children* (1937), stories of rural Mississippi, conceived and written while he lived in Chicago.

In addition to Wright, whom Robert Bone calls "the guiding spirit" of the writing group, a "literary fraternity" of approximately twenty other enthusiastic poets, novelists and playwrights were participants in the group.[8] The theoretical discussions initiated by the group often centered on the question of the "relation of the Negro writer to his folk tradition," as a means of exploring a theory of Black writing. That issue ultimately took form in Wright's classic essay "Introduction: Blueprint for Negro Writing," first published in *New Challenge* (Fall 1937). Although this new generation of Black writers wrote avidly and often in strident tones, protesting the ravages of the Depression, the painful changes wrought by the migration from their Southern homelands, and the pathology of urban life, they also wrote in celebration of the everyday folk who peopled their community of Bronzeville. Many saw their apprentice works published in the journals of the day, like *Challenge, New Challenge,* and *Negro Story* as they moved toward public recognition, literary acclaim, and the initiation of a Chicago Renaissance of Black writers.

Arna Bontemps, a frequent visitor to the writers' group, served as a bridge between the Harlem Renaissance of 1920–1935 and the Chicago Renaissance of 1935–1950; he was born in Louisiana, but lived in New York for seven years and in Chicago from 1935 to 1943. Between 1924 and 1931, his poetry won prizes in *Crisis* and *Opportunity,* prominent literary magazines of the Harlem Renaissance, yet Bontemps is most widely recognized for the prose fiction he published during the years of the Chicago Renaissance, especially *Black Thunder* (1936), a story loosely based on the Gabriel Prosser slave revolt, in Virginia in 1800. Additionally, Bontemps published *God Sends Sunday* (1931) and *Drums at Dusk* (1939).[9]

Other novelists of the Chicago Renaissance included William Attaway who published *Let Me Breathe Thunder* (1939) but is more widely known for *Blood on the Forge* (1941), a novel of the Great Migration and a protest against America's treatment of its Black minority, both in the rural South and the industrialized North. Williard Motley's first novel *Knock on Any Door* appeared in 1947 and though highly acclaimed, is most often noted for its concentration on a white protagonist and characters rather than the expected focus on Black themes and characterizations.

In addition to the novelists of the Chicago Renaissance, there were also notable poets. Prior to winning the Yale award for her only volume of poetry, *For My People* (1942), Margaret Walker's work appeared on the pages of *Poetry* magazine at least three times in the late 1930s. The poetry of Frank Marshall Davis was included in the early literary magazines; he was a recipient of a coveted Julius Rosenwald Fellowship in Creative Writing for his first book of poetry, *Black Man's Verse* (1935) and published three other volumes: *I Am the American Negro* (1937), *Through Sepia Eyes, Four Poems by Frank Marshall Davis* (1938), and *47th Street Poems* (1948). Theodore Ward, the representative voice of the dramatist during the Chicago Renaissance, produced his play *Big White Fog* (1938) with the support of the Chicago unit of the Federal Theatre Project. The impressive outpouring of literary works by Wright, Bontemps, Attaway, Motley, Walker, Davis, and Ward helped them to secure central positions on the literary stage of the Chicago Renaissance.

Likewise, Gwendolyn Brooks' considerable poetic talent assured her a well-deserved seat among her peers. At the age of thirteen, she published her first poem, "Eventide," in *American Childhood*, October 1930 and created her own newspaper, the *Champlain Weekly News*, which sold for a nickel. By age seventeen, she was a weekly contributor to the *Chicago*

Defender's "Lights and Shadows" column, beginning with her poem "To the Hinderer." In 1937, her poem "Reunion" was published in *Crisis*, and she published regularly in journals, like *Negro Story*, *Common Ground*, and *New Challenge* in the late 1930s and 1940s.[10] Brooks received national attention when she won two war bonds in a literary contest sponsored by *Negro Story* and the United Electrical Workers, AFL–CIO, for her poem "Revision of the Invocation," which was published in the May/June 1945 issue of the journal. During the 1940s, the years of World War II, Brooks' early poetry, much of which formed the core of her first book, *A Street In Bronzeville* (1945), had appeared in the *Chicago Defender*.

Along with the literary environment initiated by Vivian Harsh and nurtured by Richard Wright, a third factor in Brooks' preparation for her career as a poet occurred in 1941 when Inez Cunningham Stark, a fashionable Gold Coast socialite, critic, lecturer, president of the University of Chicago's Renaissance Society from 1936 to 1940, and patron of *Poetry* magazine, began instructing young Black aspiring poets at the South Side Community Art Center. For nearly a year, Gwendolyn Brooks Blakely, Henry Blakely II, Margaret Taylor Goss Burroughs, James Couch, Margaret Danner Cunningham, Fern Gayden, and Robert Davis were among the eager participants. Although Brooks had already received attention for her published short stories and poetry, her tutelage under Stark produced positive results. In October 1944, she won first prize in a poetry contest sponsored by Stark, and her poetry appeared on the pages of *Poetry* magazine October 1944; when she won the Midwestern Writers' Conference Award (1943), at the age of twenty-six, both Knopf and Harper publishing houses expressed interest in reviewing a complete volume of poetry by Brooks that culminated in the publication of *A Street In Bronzeville* (1945) by Harper. Thus her training under Stark clearly marks the beginning of the national acclaim that followed and thrust her in the national limelight with the

Pulitzer Prize in 1950. As with her 1945 volume of poetry, Brooks continues to approach her poetic canon as a regionalist, focusing on Chicago's South Side and especially the "Black Belt," her own community of Bronzeville.

By the 1940s Bronzeville was a teeming metropolis of urban ghetto dwellers on the South Side of Chicago. Its geographic parameters touched 28th Street on the northern and 63rd Street on the southern borders; the western line of demarcation was clearly and stringently State Street, while its eastern border followed a line that wavered along Lake Shore Drive to 47th Street, Dr. Martin Luther King Drive (originally South Park Boulevard) to 63rd Street, and finally, Cottage Grove Avenue to 67th Street (which included Washington Park from 55th to 57th Streets and a brief stretch of land from 63rd to 67th, from King Drive to Cottage Grove).[11] In their definitive sociological study of Chicago's "Black Metropolis," St. Clair Drake and Horace Cayton aptly describe Bronzeville as "a narrow tongue of land, seven miles in length and one and one-half miles in width, where more than 300,000 Negroes are packed solidly..." (12).

Although the spatial pattern of Bronzeville delineated its physical landscape, that was but a whisper of this self-contained "Black-Belt." In his sociological research which culminated in *The Negro Family in Chicago*, E. Franklin Frazier was the first to differentiate statistically by "zones" just how tight was this urban Black Belt and how restricted were the movements of its poverty-stricken inhabitants, most of whom lingered about the lowest rung of the socioeconomic ladder. His study gives credence to the reality of the great metropolis of Chicago as a concentric circle where movements were controlled by economic resources and of Bronzeville as the least mobile segment of that metropolis.[12]

The more recent arrivals to the city, European immigrants from abroad in search of employment and housing and Southern migrants fleeing the ravages of the boll weevil, bare subsistence, and blatant racism, eagerly accepted the least desirable housing in the city's central locations. With the help of low-paying factory and labor jobs created by burgeoning industrialization, the European immigrants soon learned the pattern of moving in, moving up, and moving out to the better, more stabilized far western and southern borders.[13] However, for the Black residents of Bronzeville, life was not to be so simple, so methodical, so measurable. Even when the demands of World War I dictated and European immigrants were not so plentiful, and thus among the first to be chosen for the highly paid jobs requiring skill, Black unskilled workers from the South were still last hired, first fired, and least paid among all laborers. Thus, the opportunity to shed themselves of the poverty, filth, and stagnation hovering over Bronzeville, was limited to the few professionals—doctors, lawyers, business persons—whose higher incomes paved a new road of escape which led to the more affluent residential areas—outside of Bronzeville. Otherwise, as Drake and Cayton note, most Bronzeville residents "hit the invisible barbed-wire fence of restrictive covenants. The fence may be moved back a little here and there, but never fast enough nor far enough" (382).

The "fence" that restrained the Black residents of Bronzeville was built of two very resistant and resilient materials: economic deprivation and white racism. In 1940 the evidences of Northern white racism in America were widespread in the unwritten Jim Crow practices of segregated housing, and thus, education, as well as in the limited access to equal opportunity employment. White resistance to Black intrusion was swift and pointed; Blacks who ventured, uninvited and unwelcomed, into white residential areas were immediately and uniformly bombarded with the overt hostility of property defacement, racial slurs, and physical attacks, as a prime example to other Bronzeville hopefuls that integration was *not* the theme of the day.[14] Thus, the residents of Bronzeville were forced, by their limited capacity to relocate and the crystalline rejection of white America, to create a community that provided them with a positive sense of identification, an environment that spoke to their collective cultural identities, and institutions which afforded them the sense of belonging that the larger white metropolis of Chicago did not offer.

The ethos of Bronzeville was finally created and captured by the editor of the Chicago *Bee* newspaper in 1930 when he sponsored a contest to elect a "Mayor of Bronzeville."[15] That instance of "naming" and self-identification gave birth to a community in isolation, a community which was but a microcosm of the larger dominate white society that had rejected it, and thus restricted it from full access to the American Dream. The Bronzeville residents responded by turning their combined intellectual and civic energies inward to create a community of businessmen to serve as elected "Mayors" who would act as their representative voice in the public affairs of the city at large, as well as initiate community events, such as the annual Bronzeville parade, to establish pride in their community.

The landscape of the Bronzeville community was sprinkled with a profusion of small businesses, including grocery stores, restaurants, pool halls, taverns, and cabaret clubs that invited the business of common laborers and domestics, members of the "sporting world," and local business persons and civic leaders. Also, there was a plethora of churches of varied denominations for the residents to assert their individual religious beliefs. In the 1940s Bronzeville could easily boast of the Regal Theater, the Savoy Ballroom, Provident Hospital, the George Cleveland Hall Library, and the Parkway Community House among its most famous institutions.[16]

Additionally, artist Archibald Motley, Jr. vividly depicted the sights and scenes of Bronzeville and captured some semblance of reality in a segment of Bronzeville life. In the early decades of the twentieth century, Motley turned his attention to the community of Bronzeville and concentrated on the "sporting life" of cabarets, back room gambling, and street activity in general. Contrary to the full gamut of survival methodologies adopted by the Bronzeville residents, or the five "Axes of Life" as depicted by Drake and Cayton, "Staying Alive," "Enjoying Life," "Praising the Lord," "Getting Ahead," and "Advancing the Race," Motley opted to use his artistic talents to depict only the most colorful and vibrant aspects of Black life in Bronzeville—"Enjoying Life" and "Praising the Lord" (Drake and Cayton 385).[17] Though his portraitures concentrate on a limited spectrum of life in Bronzeville, especially nightlife, they do epitomize the separate and distinct world the residents created for themselves external to their need to pursue the more serious ventures of economic, political, and social equality in America.

Similar to the sociological landscape of the community of Bronzeville as drawn by Drake and Cayton, and the artistic portraitures of Motley, Gwendolyn Brooks paints poetic portraits of her community—blueprints of urban Black life in America. Brooks' vested interest in Bronzeville stems from her nearly life time residency on Chicago's South Side and one-time residency in Bronzeville, quite similar to those of Cayton and Motley.[18] Thus, although she employs the formal distance and objectivity of an impersonal narrator in her poems, in reality, her art is a depiction of the humanity of friends, acquaintances, and neighbors, who, in a riven America, strive to survive the imposed conditions of segregation and discrimination. In these early works, *A Street In Bronzeville* (1945), *Annie Allen* (1949), and *The Bean Eaters* (1960), Brooks looks at and writes about, not a static community, but one in flux, a community that reacts and responds to the dictates of America's economic, social, and political strategies that facilitate the racial segregation and cultural isolation of Bronzeville.

Chapter II

A Street In Bronzeville (1945): A Blueprint of America's Urban Landscape

A Street in Bronzeville (1945) is Gwendolyn Brooks' poetic sketch-book of "life in the raw" for Black Americans in the urban ghetto of Bronzeville (*RPO* 133).[1] The compilation of forty-one poems forms a collage of the racism, sexism, and classism of America in its illumination of the people who strive to survive in Bronzeville. In the background of her portraits looms the shadow of the American struggle to come to grips with its diverse population by entrapping the Black community in a stagnant environment that Richard Wright terms the "segregated channels" of Negro life.[2] The diverse critical stances adopted in the reviews following the publication of Brooks' first book of poetry attest to the realism in her depiction of this Black, urban, ghetto community.

The themes most often located by critics in 1945 point to the universality, humanism, and lack of sentimentality in Brooks' work. While the *New Yorker* notes that Brooks "writes with style, sincerity, and a minimum of sentimentality. . . her city-folk poetry is particularly fresh" (80), the *Kirkus Review* goes further and commends Brooks for verse that is "gifted, passionate, and authentic" and for choosing "strictly human themes" (306). Yet there were also critics who noticed her versatility in the use of the urban idiom as well as Euro-American language. In his *New York Times Book Review* article, Rolfe Humphries confirms Brooks' nimbleness with language when he comments, "The idiom may be local but the language is universal; Miss Brooks has a command over both the colloquial and the more austere rhythms" and he too, notes that "Miss Brooks is never sentimental, never obvious" (14). And, finally, in the *Poetry* article "Sketches from Life," Amos N. Wilder opts for a review of mixed assessments. He views the work somewhat reductively when he limits nearly half the poems to "rather unexciting vignettes of sentiment and character" and stresses that these "sure-fire or easy mark situations" are viewed as "marketable" by many poets (164). He does concede, however, that even these poems are salvaged by "some actuality of detail, freshness of image, dryness of angle or flexibility" and gives special credence to "the funeral," "The Sundays of Satin-Legs Smith," and the "Gay Chaps At The Bar" sonnet series (165).

The point of convergence for the authentic flavor, sensitive spirit, and throbbing vitality of *A Street in Bronzeville* is epitomized in the central poem of the work, "The Sundays of Satin-Legs Smith." This poem, like many others of the volume, has its antecedents both in the sociological research of St. Clair Drake and Horace Cayton and in the artistic renditions of Bronzeville by Archibald Motley, Jr. The study, *Black Metropolis*, Drake and Cayton's sociological treatise of Black life in America, or more aptly "the agony of black men in a white world," as Richard Wright phrases it, is of critical importance as it relates to the delineation of the day-to-day strategies employed by the residents of Bronzeville who strive to survive (Drake vol. I xxxv). Drake and Cayton's focus on five areas of life readily conveys "the spirit of Bronzeville" in two ways. First, the study acts as a sociological palimpsest over the poetry to show the extent to which Bronzeville was a recognized and accepted metropolis in American life, and, second, it extrapolates the specific trends of life in Bronzeville as compared to the larger Chicago metropolis. Drake and Cayton define "the dominating interests" of the Bronzeville community, or "The Axes of Life," as "Staying Alive," "Having a Good Time," "Praising God," "Getting Ahead," and "Advancing the Race."[3] The axes function as a broad system of classification that, to a large extent, illuminates the concentration of energy in the community. Similarly, Motley's artistic renditions of Bronzeville's sporting life and praying life, in paintings like "Black Belt" and "Gettin' Religion," dramatize the community spirit as defined in *Black Metropolis.* Finally, while many of Brooks' poems can be categorically aligned to the residents of Bronzeville who try to stay alive, have a little fun, and attend to their spiritual needs, it is the central poem "The Sundays of Satin-Legs Smith" that encompasses all three of these major axes.[4]

As a powerful statement on the oppressive conditions facing the residents of Bronzeville, the poignant portrayal of Satin-Legs is augmented by vignettes of the places and people who strive to survive in Bronzeville by "working hard," "having a good time," and "praising the Lord." The fact that Brooks' characters are not depicted either "Getting Ahead" or "Advancing the Race" is in itself an implicit social commentary of the dire times and conditions of Bronzeville. However, Brooks does make three major and explicit statements of social commentary in *A Street in Bronzeville;* she examines the physical deterioration of the tenements in Bronzeville, the limited options for Black women, and the ambivalence of Black men fighting the dual wars for democracy and equality.

First, Brooks constructs an urban landscape in the poem "kitchenette building," which informs Satin-Legs' dreary place of residence. The sense of place gains increasing clarity in the poems "the soft man," "patent leather," and "the independent man," all of which elaborate upon the theme of Satin-Legs' involvement in the night life of Bronzeville and his sexual pursuits. In the poems "Matthew Cole" and "of De Witt Williams on his way to Lincoln Cemetery," as the poet mourns De Witt's lowly origins in his funeral elegy, she also mirrors the bleakness of Satin-Legs' life and foreshadows the doom of his final days.

Secondly, the poet captures vivid portraits of the women of Bronzeville. In character vignettes like "Sadie and Maud," "The Queen of the Blues," "the mother," "the ballad of chocolate Mabbie," "Ballad of Pearl May Lee," and the "Hattie Scott" series, it becomes clear that Black women of the 1940s were faced with limited economic opportunities, intraracial color hierarchies, and spousal abuse, as well as racism, sexism, and classism. And in a final statement of social commentary, the poet takes a global perspective of war. Brooks expands the perception of America's racial disparities and the extent to which those disparities create divisiveness in America's military troops in the poems "Negro Hero" and the "Gay Chaps At The Bar" sonnet series. Thus, this sequence of poems from *A Street in Bronzeville*, beginning with "kitchenette building," defines the veil of oppression that stretches across the lives of the Bronzeville residents and forcibly restrains them.

For instance, in "kitchenette building," Brooks recreates the period of the 1930s and '40s when the old mansions on Chicago's South Side were turned into exorbitantly priced tenement buildings to house the desperate residence seekers from the South. To accommodate Chicago's unwritten policy of residential segregation, poor Blacks were forced to live in former mansions which had been dissected into tiny rooms with kitchenettes.[5] The poem opens with an air of finality from a first-person communal voice that cannot conceive of such lofty abstractions as "dreams" existing amid the suffocation of their poverty stricken reality:

> We Are things of dry hours and the involuntary plan,
> Grayed in, and gray. "Dream" makes a giddy sound, not
> strong
> Like "rent," "feeding a wife," "satisfying a man." (20)

The narrator's opening statement hints at the ravages of a history of slavery ("the involuntary plan") that has left these ghetto survivors devoid of the fertility of hope ("things of dry hours") and suggests that, at best, their hopes and dreams have been diluted and cemented to the nothingness epitomized by the phrase "Grayed in, and gray."

In the second stanza, the narrator dares to hope that a dream might survive the stalking poverty and queries hesitantly, "But could a dream send up through onion fumes . . . ?" Because the narrator suspects the flimsy fabric of which "white and violet" dreams must be made, she is staunch in her contention that a battle with "fried potatoes" and "yesterday's garbage ripening in the hall" would render a dream helpless even if the residents "Had time to warm it, keep it very clean." A note of even greater clarity is sounded when the narrator elevates dreams to the stature of "an aria," yet equates the lives of the ghetto residents with rot and stench. But quickly, the bubbles of a fragile imagination are burst by the narrator's reality check, and the momentary exploration into the foreign world of hopes and dreams is thrust aside in the final tercet:

> We wonder. But not well! not for a minute!
> Since Number Five is out of the bathroom now,
> We think of lukewarm water, hope to get in it. (20)

In terms of the formal structure, the poem strains towards the regularity of iambic pentameter, but with little success. Its varied meter and irregular rhyme support the internal struggle of a speaker who would like to believe in the normalcy of dreams, even where the contrary conditions of ghetto existence belie that option. The powerful trochees "Grayed in" and "Flutter" supply ample evidence of the residents' feeling of entrapment in contrast to the whimsical quality of their dreams.[6] In "kitchenette building," the speaker's tone is one of limited hopefulness as a commentary on the impoverishment permeating urban Black America where "lukewarm water" is the ultimate aspiration of ghetto tenants.

Like "kitchenette building," the poem "the soft man" establishes a sense of place yet serves double duty as it strays across the boundaries of "having a good time" in the nightlife of Bronzeville and "praising the Lord" in the churches. The third-person judgmental narrator issues forth a tirade against one she deems "disgusting" because of his familiarity with common language and common social places. The narrator of "the soft man" is appalled at the "sweet vulgarity" of the disgusting hipster who applies stereotypical labels to women and men alike: "And calling women (Marys) chicks and broads, / Men hep, and cats, or corny to the jive" (25). Like the axes identified by Drake and Cayton, the soft man is busy:

> Being seen Everywhere (keeping Alive),
> Rhumboogie (and the joint is jumpin', Joe),
> Brass Rail, Keyhole, De Lisa, Cabin Inn.
> And all the other garbage cans. (25)

His need to frequent the "juke" joints of Bronzeville situates him in close proximity with the nightlife revisited in "of De Witt Williams on his way to Lincoln Cemetery," "The Sundays Of Satin-Legs Smith," and "Queen of the Blues."

Brooks executes a skillful turn in the second stanza of the poem that succinctly conveys the other face of "the soft man." The chagrin of the narrator is suddenly replaced by a smirking and sardonic tone as she shares the knowledge that "soft" refers to the man's need for religious salvation after his lively evening jaunts have left him spiritually depleted, and that "creep" serves double duty for what he is and what he does:

> But grin.
> Because there is a clean unanxious place
> To which you creep on Sundays. And you cool
> In lovely sadness. (25)

The tone of ironic accusation continues as the narrator smugly notes that for all his fun and games and hipness, the soft man's life of "keeping Alive" is insufficient for his survival and must be supplemented by "praising the Lord." In the final lines she juxtaposes his street life and religious life and notes that in contrast to his fun spots, no one "giggles" in church where he ventures to bathe his "sweet vulgarity in prayer."

A second poem which helps set the stage for the full-blown depiction of Satin-Legs' sexual pursuits is "patent leather," where the female chooses a replica of the Satin-Legs' persona. The opening quatrain of the poem introduces the wimpy male narrators of the poem who cannot contain their envy directed at two of the more "hip" contingency of Bronzeville who have made a romantic alliance. Their use of the urban vernacular situates them squarely in the middle of Bronzeville:

> That cool chick down on Calumet
> Has got herself a brand new cat,
> With pretty patent-leather hair.
> And he is man enough for her. (29)

The disdain they feel that one was not chosen from among their ranks is clear in the off-rhyme endings of the opening stanza above and the compression in the second stanza:

> Us other guys don't think he's such
> A much.
> His voice is shrill.
> His muscle is pitiful. (29)

The description of the cat's slick and "pretty patent leather hair" is intentionally aligned with a predominantly feminine slick and glossy fabric and suggestive of the popular waved hairstyle for men in the 1940s. That description, along with the negative characteristics attributed to him by the unsophisticated street narrators, suggests artificiality on the part of both the "new cat" and the "cool chick." Yet the partial repetition of the final line in the first and final quatrain, "That makes him man enough for her," hints not only at the envy of the male bystanders, but also acknowledges the value of the male's stunning surface attributes, like "pretty patent-leather hair," over any real intrinsic human qualities, aspirations, or accomplishments, which will be recalled in the attention Satin-Legs gives to his own physical appearance.

Brooks' continuing litany on the urban Black male finally forms a picture of men who have not attained the outer accouterments of the American Dream. They are not presented in terms of successful careers, happy family life, or full participation in the force of American life. Conversely, poems like "the independent man," "of De Witt Williams on his way to Lincoln Cemetery," and "Matthew Cole" offer relentless portraits of urban oppression. The poem "the independent man" is a continuing perusal of men whose focus is on the brief, intimate, sensual satisfactions of life, rather than any intense involvement in economic gain. Appropriately, the metaphor for an independent man is a "flask of wine" which "not a cork / Could you allow, for being made so free" (33). And in a final terse couplet, the narrator dismisses his importance: "A woman would be wise to think it well / If once a week you only rang the bell."

Unlike "the independent man," the poet / narrator in "of De Witt Williams on his way to Lincoln Cemetery" eulogizes De Witt in a low plaintive note that recalls the poignant spirituals sung by slaves. The poem becomes a social commentary on the ordinariness and finality in the lives of Black men like De Witt and Satin-Legs that belies the history of struggle preceding them.

The structure of the poem, "an exquisite, ballad-type elegy," as described by D. H. Melhem, supports allusions to the history of slavery, the sonorous tone of the Negro spirituals, and the "unimportant" death of one Black man (31). The opening quatrain and couplet foreshadow the "Satin-Legs" poem by aligning the Southern origins of De Witt to those of Satin-Legs and confirming their meager impact in the larger scheme of things:

> He was born in Alabama.
> He was bred in Illinois.
> He was nothing but a
> Plain black boy.
>
> Swing low swing low sweet sweet chariot.
> Nothing but a plain black boy. (39)

The haunting play on the old spiritual "Swing Low, Sweet Chariot" infuses the poem with the historical pain of slavery and recalls James Weldon Johnson's ambivalent reference to "These songs of sorrow, love and faith, hope" in "O Black and Unknown Bards" (11) and Du Bois' suggestion that "through all of the Sorrow Songs there breathes a hope—a faith in the ultimate justice of things...that sometime, somewhere, men will judge men by their souls and not by their skins" (186). The repetition of the first two stanzas, at the poem's end, enclose De Witt's stymied life of "having a good time" at the meager entertainment centers of Bronzeville and define his limited existence in America:

> Drive him past the Pool Hall.
> Drive him past the Show.
> Blind within his casket,
> But maybe he will know.
>
> Down through Forty-seventh Street:
> Underneath the L,
> And—Northwest Corner, Prairie,
> That he loved so well.

Don't forget the Dance Halls—
Warwick and Savoy,
Where he picked his women, where
He drank his liquid joy. (39)

The political implications of the poem emerge first in the title, which recalls Abraham Lincoln's Emancipation Proclamation; next, in the allusion to Lincoln Cemetery, where, symbolically, De Witt will be "freed" for the second time; and finally, in the repeated reference to De Witt as a "Plain black boy," at a time when the use of the term "black" could stir up serious controversy.[7] Although the seemingly controlled voice of the narrator conceals any glaring statement of social injustice, her subtle tone is one of cool reproach for the waste and loss inherent in ghetto life and thus suggests a commentary of social inequality as the ruling force of De Witt's life.

Finally, in those poems that help lay the landscape of *A Street in Bronzeville,* the poem "Matthew Cole" offers a disturbing portrait of the domestic reality faced by many residents of Bronzeville. Mere survival is the theme of "Matthew Cole." The abrupt narrator opens:

Here are the facts.
He's sixty-six.
He rooms in a stove-heated flat
Over on Lafayette. (40)

Matthew's unimportance in the world is compressed into tight little lines of dimeter and trimeter meter and constrained in the austerity of rhymeless end-stopped lines. The sparse image of the opening lines bears the implication of poverty in the "stove-heated flat" and his virtual anonymity in the vague reference to his place of residence "Over on Lafayette." The pains of Matthew's poverty-ridden life are evident in later restrained lines of the verse:

And the gloomy housekeeper
Who forgets to build the fire,
And the red fat roaches that stroll
Unafraid up his wall, (40)

The survival technique Matthew employs to endure his sad little life is the soothing salve of memory, as explained by the omniscient narrator: "He never smiles. Except when come, / Say, thoughts of a little boy licorice-full." The final lines of the poem duly expand to accommodate the richness of Matthew's memories of yesterday, which are keeping him alive today: "Once I think, he laughed aloud, / At thought of a wonderful joke he'd played / On the whole crowd, the old crowd. . . ." (40).

Just as Brooks creates poetic commentary about the social conditions affecting the lives of the Black men of Bronzeville, she also paints memorable portraits of the women in *A Street in Bronzeville.* In the 1940s Black women faced the same economic impoverishment as men, were equally stymied in terms of employment opportunities, but unique to their gender, also made emotionally wrenching decisions about their unborn children. The poems "Sadie and Maud," "Queen of the Blues," "the mother," "the ballad of chocolate Mabbie," "Ballad of Pearl May Lee," and the "Hattie Scott" series tell the stories of the ordinary women who peopled the streets of Bronzeville and the survival tactics they used to stay alive in the ghetto.

As a contrast to the entertainment life of the men of Bronzeville, like Satin-Legs and De Witt, Brooks creates vivid depictions of two of the more socially aggressive women of Bronzeville. There is an element of "having fun" in the poems "Sadie and Maud" and "Queen Of the Blues," though for the Queen, that fun is tinged with sexism. Interestingly, the fact that the first two lines of "Sadie and Maud" are end-stopped sets up a definitive dichotomy between one who is expected to "get ahead," versus one who is representative of her Bronzeville counterparts, few of whom have an escape from the stifling ghetto environment:

> Maud went to college.
> Sadie stayed at home. (16)

The first hint that Maud's lofty aspirations have not come to fruition appears in the third stanza of the five-stanza ballad. The only stanza to alter the pattern of quatrains, by employing repetition and expanding the story-line in a six-line variation, this stanza subtly informs the reader that Maud has somehow returned home, and instead of being aligned with her sister Sadie, has now joined the ranks of their parents:

> Sadie bore two babies
> Under her maiden name.
> Maud and Ma and Papa
> Nearly died of shame.
> Every one but Sadie
> Nearly died of shame. (32)

It is not until the final stanza that it becomes clear that indeed Maud has replaced the parents and "Is a thin brown mouse. / She is living alone / In this old house."

Conversely, Sadie manages, for a time, not only to survive, but live life to the fullest. Metaphorically, she "scraped life / With a fine-tooth comb" without leaving "a tangle in"; she scraped the bottom of life's barrel with no remorse and is profiled as "one of the livingest chits/In all the land." Unlike Maud, who adheres to the societal norm of pursuing education to "get ahead" and thereby derive a better life, Sadie opts to extract the very flavor of life on her own terms and according to her poetic legacy survives and has a good time. The measure of her success is evident in the heritage she bequeaths to her daughters—"Her fine-tooth comb."

Brooks uses a circular structure to set up the polarities of the contrasting faces of societal norms. The ballad begins and ends with Maud, only to show her futile attempts to grasp the means of a "better" life. Brooks exploits the structure of the ballad form just as Sadie has thwarted societal norms and conveys Sadie's satisfaction by using repetition in the third stanza: "Everyone but Sadie / Nearly died of shame." When Brooks returns to the traditional quatrain format in the last two stanzas, what was first seen as unusual is now acceptable; Sadie's daughters have adopted her survival strategies and "struck out from home," and Maud, "a thin brown mouse," has returned home.

Like Sadie, Mame in "Queen Of The Blues" is a survivor, but unlike Sadie, Mame is not having a good time; by contrast, her role is to provide a good time for others. The play on "the queen of the blues" recalls the history of and poetic tributes to early blues stars like Bessie Smith, "Ma" Rainey, and Billie Holiday, whose own struggles to survive were second to the balm their blues songs provided for others. Poets often pay tribute to the trials of blues queens in poems like Robert Hayden's "Homage to the Empress of the Blues" and Sterling Brown's "Ma Rainey."[8]

"Queen Of The Blues," like "the soft man" and "of De Witt Williams on his way to Lincoln Cemetery," targets the show places and clubs in Bronzeville where folks can go to relieve the pain of their weary lives; yet only in the opening stanza is there a hint, though short-lived, of revelry for the queen:

Mame was singing
At the Midnight Club.
And the place was red
With blues.
She could shake her body
Across the floor.
For what did she have
To lose? (56)

The meager expectation for the queen to have a good time is offset by the sparse lines of the ballad and its terse language. The symbolism of vibrant red as lively abandon is cut to the quick by the resounding smack of the next line, which abruptly focuses on the "blues." For Mame not only sings the blues, she has the blues. The remainder of the ballad variation recounts not her blues songs, but her blues filled life; her "mama" is dead, she has no "Legal pa," no "Big brother," "small brother," "Baby girl" or "Sonny boy" to make her feel the shame of her profession. Her sole blues lament, accented with blues repetition, is that she cannot find "a man / What will love me / Till I die." The queen alludes to the sore consequences of her romantic alliances when she substitutes a sugar "daddy" for real parental authority. The "daddy" she was good to and loved "Found him a brown-skin chicken," after she "gave him all of [her] dough" that she earned by scrubbing floors in "white folks'" Kitchens."

The only recognition and accolade the queen gets is from the emcee, and even he limits the bounds of her "Queen" stature to that of a blues star by introducing her as "Queen of the blues! / Strictly, strictly, / The queen of the blues!" The irony of her title is evident in her final query:

> Men are low down
> Dirty and mean.
> Why don't they tip
> Their hats to a queen? (59)

Brooks' women, like the "Queen of the Blues" are alive and vibrant as they struggle against the racism, sexism, classism that invade their lives.

One of Brooks' most memorable character vignettes is a poignant portrayal of a mother who understands the responsibilities of her life and meets them head on, even in the face of her own grief. In "the mother," Brooks creates a dramatic monologue to permit the ghetto mother of an aborted child to tell her own story of loss. It is amazingly ironic that the poem is still deemed one of Brooks' most powerful poems given the searing social statement it makes about a topic which, historically, has caused major dissension in America.[9] But Brooks' speaker endears herself to the reader by assuming full responsibility for her act and sharing the inner trauma that will be her very own infinite pain.

The speaker opens the poem in an inchoate second-person voice as she haltingly broaches a topic that in the 1940s seldom found a receptive audience:

> Abortions will not let you forget.
> You remember the children you got that you did not
>   get,
> The damp small pulps with a little or with no hair, (21)

Once the mother finds her own sorrowful voice and lingers over a haunting description of her lost children, she acknowledges, in a forlorn tone, that she can never "Return for a snack of them, with gobbling mother-eye." The emotional momentum of the telling is a psychological breakthrough for the anguished mother, who finds the strength, in the second verse, to take ownership of her deed and her pain. She reveals: "I have heard in the voices of the wind the voices of my dim killed children." The vague "you" of the opening stanza is now "I" as the mother moves from telling the sense of absence that will torment another to claiming the pain of maternal absence as her own. She embraces her body as the intended vessel for the aborted child in lines that may stunningly be likened to the act of childbirth:

> I have contracted. I have eased
> My dim dears at the breasts they could never suck. (21)

And once the flood-gate opens, mother-memories gush through as she considers that if she has "sinned," her "crime" was not as intentional as it was necessary; she states: "Believe that even in my deliberateness I was not deliberate." And, finally, the mother makes an impassioned plea to her unborn children to believe that in spite of her deed, she did love them:

> Believe me, I loved you all.
> Believe me, I knew you, though faintly, and I loved, I
> loved you
> All. (22)

The haunting refrains of a ghetto mother whose own struggle to survive will not permit her to support a new life is supported by the formal structure of the poem. The shifting metrical pattern of the poem parallels the junctures where the mother struggles, thoughtfully, to examine her own feelings about the abortion. The sudden reversal from iambic to anapestic meter in the repetition of "You will never," "I have heard," "I have contracted," and "I have said" illuminate the magnitude of the mother's loss. The use of rhymed couplets to convey information about the aborted child signals the memories associated with childlike melodies while the lines that point to the child's death are more somber and devoid of rhyme.

In a differing angle of the racial trials of the Black community, viewed from a gender perspective, Brooks makes a social commentary on the pain caused by both intraracial and interracial color hierarchies. In "the ballad of chocolate Mabbie" and the "Ballad Of Pearl May Lee," the poet examines the romantic inclinations of two very different females and how color impacts the individual outcomes. These poems attest to the intraracial color complex in the Black community and the fact that it nearly mirrors the interracial color discrimination initiated by the dominant white society. In "The Black-and-Tan Motif in the Poetry of Gwendolyn Brooks," Arthur Davis discusses the friction, misunderstanding, heartache, and tragedy that are the painful outcomes of this color divisiveness and make life "particularly difficult for the dark girl" (90). Davis quotes a common joke among Black men of the community to illustrate the stark reality of color hierarchies:

> Yaller gal rides in an automobile;
> Brown gal rides the train.
> Black gal rides in an ol' ox cart,
> But she gets there jes the same. (Davis 90)

In "the ballad of chocolate Mabbie," Brooks exerts considerable artistic control to capture the optimism in the lofty air of childhood expectations, as well as the dismal cloud of disappointment in the clearing of reality. Contrary to Gary Smith's contention that Mabbie's life is one of "unrelieved monotony," the opening stanza of the six-quatrain ballad nearly bursts with Mabbie's enthusiasm for life (50):

> It was Mabbie without the grammar school gates.
> And Mabbie was all of seven.
> And Mabbie was cut from a chocolate bar.
> And Mabbie thought life was heaven. (30)

The connotation of "battle" that is subtly injected in the title is reinforced by the fact that the poem denotes Mabbie's resilience as she wages a war against reality in pursuit of her own happiness. Similarly, anaphora, effectively used above and in the repetition of "Mabbie on Mabbie" in the last stanza, heightens the reflection of Mabbie's idealism in a world she feels has been created to deliver her share of life's bliss. An optimistic air rings throughout the first three stanzas and hints at the possibility that Mabbie will be judged on the merits of her internal, rather than external qualities. For Mabbie, "The grammar school gates were the pearly gates" that would soon release her heart throb, "Willie Boone."

In the fourth quatrain, Brooks departs from the folksy chant of the ballad form and improvises with the lyrical voice of the third-person omniscient speaker to convey the true heights of ecstasy to which little Mabbie has soared in an imagination that knows no bounds:

> Oh, warm is the waiting for joys, my dears!
> And it cannot be too long.
> Oh, pity the little poor chocolate lips
> That carry the bubble of song! (30)

Yet in that third line, the narrator foreshadows the doom of Mabbie's dreams. When the "saucily bold Willie Boone" finally emerges from school, it is not to join Mabbie, for "He wore like a jewel a lemon-hued lynx / With sand-waves loving her brow." In a posture that evokes visions of Daniel Boone, Willie has the aura of a hunter, who proudly displays his quarry. In the final lines of the poem, when Mabbie is left "alone by the grammar school gates" with only the camaraderie of her "chocolate companions," there is a distinct sense of finality, suggesting that the caste system, as delineated by skin color, informs the intraracial color hierarchy.[10]

Likewise, though thematically the "Ballad Of Pearl May Lee" tackles the subject of lynching as the outcome of an interracial sexual liaison, it is also a tale of dual revenge since its secondary motif is clear in the tragic overtones of an enraged woman who has been ostracized by a man, based solely on her dark hue. Pearl declares that her man, Sammy, has been hauled "off to the jail" and, later, "wrapped . . . around a cottonwood tree" because of his obsession with a white woman:

> Then a white girl passed you by one day,
> And, the vixen, she gave you the wink.
> And your stomach got sick and your legs liquefied.

And you thought till you couldn't think.
  You thought,
  You thought,
You thought till you couldn't think. (61, 62)

Pearl notes that even in school Sammy's choices were "the bright little girls" and that he "couldn't abide dark meat . . . Black was for the famished to eat." So when Sammy stumbles upon a woman who is "white like milk," he is unable to resist. But, in his surrender to the woman, whose "breasts were cups of cream," lay Sammy's demise when the woman screams rape.

Formally, Brooks does not confine her verse to a strict ballad stanza, nor does she adhere to a strict *aab* rhyme scheme of the two-part three-line blues form. Instead, she melds the narrative framework of the ballad with the distinct ethos of the blues to enlarge the landscape of the tale. Although each of the sixteen stanzas is composed of an initial four-line ballad stanza with the *abcb* rhyme scheme, each stanza ends with either a repeating blues couplet of *cb* or a three-line closing refrain that nearly replicates the three-line blues form in *bbb* or *ddb.*

Brooks' incorporation of the repetition of the blues refrain into a ballad stanza produces a form that is sufficiently expansive to encompass a historically grounded tale that can bear the double tragedy of race and romance.[11] The repetition in Pearl's song points to her case of the "blues" in the face of romantic rejection, but, even as she sings a song of jubilant revenge, she wails her own loss in the mournful strains of the blues:

Oh, dig me out of my don't-despair.
Oh, pull me out of my poor-me.
Oh, get me a garment of red to wear.
You had it coming surely.
  Surely.
  Surely.
You had it coming surely. (63)

Though the theme of intraracial and interracial color hierarchies is addressed in only two poems of Brooks' first volume of poetry, it is one that resurfaces both in *Annie Allen* and *The Bean Eaters.* In "The Anniad," Annie views herself as an "unembroidered brown" (100), and in "XIII / Intermission, 3," a woman is admonished: "Stand off, daughter of the dusk. / And do not wince when the bronzy lads / Hurry to cream-yellow shining" (137), both from *Annie Allen.* Similarly, the color hierarchies evident in the poems "Jesse Mitchell's Mother" (344) and "Bronzeville Woman in a Red Hat" (367), from *The Bean Eaters*, are testament to the prevalence of the intraracial and interracial color complex in America.[12]

In her continuing emphasis on the lives of Black women, Brooks' "Hattie Scott" series depicts several facets of one woman's existence which serve as particular examples of the limited employment opportunities available to Black women in the first quarter of this century. Elise Johnson McDougald adds historical credence to Brooks' poetic depiction when she assesses the economic handicaps of Black women of the early 1900s in "The Task of Negro Womanhood." The economic limitations that encumbered Black women become easily discernible when viewed through the prism of the ascending numbers of women in the less desirable occupations. McDougald classifies Black women in the leisure group, business and professions, trades and industry, and finally, the most weighted group—those involved in menial labor and domestic services as maids and housekeepers.[13] When explicated against the backdrop of these economic constraints, the "Hattie Scott" series becomes a microcosm of life for Black women in urban America.

This series of character vignettes signifies economic exploitation, America's white standards of beauty, and spousal abuse as factors in the Black woman's life that contribute to her repressed rage. The use of the interior monologue is an especially effective means of conveying the thoughts of an urban Black woman in her own idiom, versus the standard English language which is Brooks' predominate vernacular in the volume. Brooks plays against the ballad form in her insistent use of the *abcb* stanzaic pattern and thus suggests the historic importance of Hattie Scott as the archetypal frustrated Black female domestic worker. The series can be aligned effectively with "Negro Hero" in the seemingly diverse domestic and military roles, which, by limiting Black men and women to the most menial chores, keep them confined to the bottom rung of America's economic ladder.

The initial poem, "the end of the day," signals Hattie's confinement in the opening line: "It's usually from the insides of the door / That I takes my peek at the sun" and follows up on that theme in a later line with subtle internal rhyme: "...Not ...that I couldn't / Sneak out on the back porch a bit." Metaphorically, Hattie likens her daily drudgery to that of the sun since, at the end of the day they both "Cap the job, then to hell with it." Like the frustrated worker in Claude McKay's sonnet, "The Tired Worker," who views "The wretched day" as his enemy, in Brooks' poem, the Hattie Scott persona mourns the return of the sun because "Then it's wearily back for me" (51).

A second vignette, "the date," extends the exploration of Hattie's life as a domestic when Hattie, in her interior monologue, conceals her belligerence from her "fool" of an employer, for fear of economic reprisal. Brooks evokes a sense of tension by constraining Hattie's wrath in two tightly woven unbroken stanzas that demonstrate Hattie's irritability at the endless array of chores blocking the path to her date. Hattie's bellicose tone effectively conveys her distaste for her adversarial employer and the sense of entrapment she acknowledges in her internal rage:

> If she don't hurry up and let me out of here.
> Keeps pilin' up stuff for me to do.
> I ain't goin' to finish that ironin'.

She got another think comin'. Hey, you. (52)

In one of Brooks' poetic hallmarks—her abruptness of speech—she polishes off Hattie's monologue with a spondaic flourish in the final couplet of the poem: "I'm leavin'. Got somethin' interestin' on my mind. / Don't mean night school."

The third poem of the "Hattie Scott" series, "at the hairdressers," considers a topic which gains increasing momentum throughout Brooks' poetic canon—the subject of Black women's hair. Endowed with a head of short hair, Hattie Scott confronts the issue of self-acceptance in a society whose definition of glamour celebrates an image of long flowing tresses. The negative effects of this stereotypical standard of beauty wreak havoc upon Hattie's psyche.

Again, the ballad format works to sing of the plight of Black women as mirror images of the insecurities Hattie faces, while the use of the urban idiom and the hip syncopated rhythms situate Hattie squarely outside white America. In the opening of four stanzas, a cocky Hattie demands of her beautician:

Gimmie an upsweep, Minnie,
With humpteen baby curls.
Bout time I got some glamour.
I'll show them girls. (53)

But, after admitting to her failed attempts to increase her hair length, by using "Madam C. J. Walker's" and "Poro Grower" hairdressings, Hattie's confidence dwindles in her ability to compete with the "fly a-struttin girls" whose hair is like "wool a-blowin' 'round." Her hesitancy is clear in the third stanza when she asks: "Long hair's out of style anyhow, ain't it?" Hattie's plaintive question is a social commentary on Black America's obsession with white beauty standards and the emotional havoc wreaked upon a community of women who feel unable to meet those standards.[14]

In a continuing look at life in Bronzeville from the perspective of women, the final two poems in the "Hattie Scott" series, "when I die" and "the battle," tell of the frail attempts of human beings to survive life's daily traumas. In "when I die," Hattie does not mourn her own death, but admits to her minor importance in a world where "No lodge with banners flappin' / Will follow after me." Instead, she caringly describes the "shabbily" dressed "little short man" who does care enough to escort her to her grave. It is a poignant portrayal of a man whose dire poverty permits him to show his affection by laying "his buck-a-dozen" flowers on "with care" and who is rewarded by "angels" who will "be watchin', / And kiss him sweetly there" as a confirmation of his innate goodness. But, finally, the man's survival will be placed in the hands of "the girls" who will be waiting to capture his affections once he "wipe[s] his tears away." And, having ascertained that he will survive after all, Hattie's final words are, "There's nothin' more to say" (38).

The final poem of the series, "the battle," is a tale of gossip and intrigue, where the third-person speaker shares what she has heard—"Her landlady told my ma"—about another woman's domestic affairs. The poem is an account of, in the urban vernacular, "a knock-down-drag-out fight" between Moe Belle Jackson, and her abusive husband. Ironically, the poem turns on the subtle suggestion that Moe Belle "probably" "shed a tear" of contrition to her husband the morning after the battle, and the chagrin of the female narrator is fueled by her seemingly personal knowledge of Moe Belle's past submissive responses to her violent husband. Thus, in the second of three quatrains, the narrator reflects on her own hypothetical responses to such a battle:

> I like to think
> Of how I'd of took a knife
> And slashed all of the quickenin'
> Out of his lowly life. (55)

The poem signals the silent acceptance of abuse by women whose very survival in such situations depends upon their submissiveness. The speaker spews out the anger, hostility, and repression of such women as a suggestion of the psychological aggression that may be a seething caldron beneath the veneer of humility. In the final stanza, the full vent of the speaker's wrath is easily detected as she reduces Moe Belle to a mere victim who "shed a tear," resumes her position of servility, and the next day asks her husband at breakfast, "More grits, dear?"

The "Hattie Scott" series and other poems that capture the lives of women in *A Street in Bronzeville* are crucial evidence of Brooks' early attention to women's issues and her comfort level in making social statements about a wide range of women's activities, including religion, blues singing, and abortion. Brooks sees her community in its totality—the men, the women, the children—and broaches, unafraid, the every-day-ness of their lives, devoid of any attempt to extrapolate them by gender or polarize them. The effectiveness of her poetry about women is the supreme distance she assumes in order to let these women tell their own stories of how America's oppressive conditions impact their lives. In her women's poems, as in all her poetry, Brooks' character vignettes can stand alone and tell their own intimate stories without her personal intervention.[15] Even in the most powerful, male-centered work of the collection, "The Sundays of Satin-Legs Smith," a woman sits at the crest of Satin-Leg's day and is the recipient of his lavish preparations for an evening of pleasure.

Thematically, stylistically, and aesthetically, "The Sundays of Satin-Legs Smith" is the pivotal poem of *A Street in Bronzeville* that epitomizes the lived experience of the Black male in the urban setting of Bronzeville. In a circular structure, the poem revolves around a day in the life of a Black, male ghetto dweller. Brooks insistently probes the dire economic deprivation of Bronzeville in the major work of the volume as a continued social commentary on the racial disparities existing in America. Although the period of the 1940s generally rode the crest of a wave of optimism brought in by the aftermath of World War II programs, such as President Roosevelt's New Deal and Works Progress Administration, little of that optimism filtered down to Bronzeville's Black underclass, many of whom were unskilled Southern migrants.

In a stroke of narrative dexterity, Brooks expertly deploys a judgmental speaker to Bronzeville who has the cultural propensity to peruse Satin-Legs' urban environment from a dual perspective. The educated third-person, omniscient narrator artfully weaves a tale for a silent, white observer that situates the deplorable economic conditions of Satin-Legs' poverty-stricken community against the more highly touted cultural ambiance of European society. Because Satin-Legs is not fully cognizant of the origins of the economic deprivation that holds his community hostage, he cannot navigate the observer through the troubled waters of his oppressive existence. Thus, it is the educated narrator who conveys Satin-Legs' oblivion to any but his own meager survival concerns and explores his subconscious thought processes by lacing them into her own intimate knowledge of ghetto life. The outcome of this narrative technique is that it yields a more perceptive analysis of Satin-Legs' life than he can supply in his own first-person voice.

Critic Onwuchekwa Jemie duly notes Brooks' generally indeterminate tone and her ambivalent attitude toward Satin, which "ranges from scorn and disapprobation to admiration," yet fails to discern the narrative strategy she employs to unfold the rich character profile of Satin-Legs (168). Theoretically, the narrator espouses the socio-political tenets of W. E. B. Du Bois by announcing her presence in the lofty idiom of a "talented tenth" class affiliate in the opening line of the poem:

> INAMORATAS, with an approbation,
> Bestowed his title. Blessed his inclination. (42)

The narrator possesses a "double-consciousness" born of a Euro-American, privileged sensibility, which is at odds with the low socioeconomic status of the ghetto dwellers of Bronzeville. The expressive voice of the narrator signals the ambivalence of Du Bois' American Negro who ever feels his "twoness,—an American, a Negro; two souls, two thoughts, two unreconciled strivings; two warring ideals in one dark body, whose dogged strength alone keeps it from being torn asunder."[16] Thus, as the narrator strives to convey the subtle nuances of Satin-Legs' ghetto existence to an apparently opinionated, silent, white observer, she vacillates between the genteel poise she exhibits on her elevated educational perch and the awkward stance she adopts on the lowly stoop of Bronzeville, as she defends Satin-Legs' right to define his own existence in an environment where the pervasiveness of racism in America sets the tenor of his life. What Jemie finally misses is Brooks' superb technical device of creating a narrator who can negotiate a literary excursion into the deepest realms of both the African American and the Euro-American consciousness to tell the full story of a Black man who insistently defines himself against the backdrop of his own community and remains stoically oblivious to the social realism of the larger, white American scene.[17]

In contrast to the class-conscious narrator, Satin-Legs represents the epitome of identity in a society that denies him a positive definition. Rather than succumb to "a world which yields him no true self-consciousness, but only lets him see himself through the revelation of the other world," Satin-Legs has formulated his own identity and is blind to the attempts of others to define him by their own cultural clarity (Du Bois 3). By virtue of America's denial of his full participation in the social equality of the larger society, Satin-Legs has little choice but to formulate his own sense of cultural interiority, which is revealed in the astute analysis of the narrator.[18]

The myriad illusions of Satin-Legs' life begin with the

amorous women who suggestively highlight his sensuality by naming him in terms of doting affection; thus, when he awakens and stretches into his royal posture, it is in keeping with an established persona:

> He wakes, unwinds, elaborately: a cat
> Tawny, reluctant, royal. He is fat
> And fine this morning. Definite. Reimbursed. (42)

Contrary to Gary Smith's view that Satin-Legs is embarking upon a "largely purposeless Sunday outing," Satin-Legs actually has a mental itinerary for his day that centers around "having a good time" (Mythologies 46). From Satin-Legs' perspective, indulging in the activities of Bronzeville's "sporting life," as exemplified by the activities of the earlier poems "the soft man" and "the independent man," and the past haunts catalogued in "of De Witt Williams on his way to Lincoln Cemetery," having a good time *is* the purpose of Sunday. Because Satin-Legs' world rotates around the axis of his stunning surface qualities, rather than any captivating intellectual charisma, he "designs his reign" with a "performance" that is geared, in the urban vernacular, "to catch" the Bronzeville women. The apex of his outing is the intimate time he shares with his selected lady even though his "spat-out purchased kisses" signify his female companions as prostitutes. Satin-Legs rises in an oxymoronic "clear delirium" that emanates from the "remnants of last night's high life and distress," and sallies forth to embark upon a new day of having a good time.[19]

The omniscient narrator reveals that Satin-Legs "sheds, with his pajamas, shabby days," although Satin-Legs, in his coolly nonchalant demeanor, never acknowledges any conscious feelings of the "desertedness," "fear," "postponed resentments," or "prim precautions" she asserts on his behalf. It is this duality in the narrator's consciousness that permits the observer to peek behind the "veil" that shuts Satin-Legs out from full participation in the American Dream; as Melhem states: "respectable life [is] closed to him" (33). Formally, the narrator establishes Satin-Legs' persona in an opening rhymed couplet, then expands it in three tercets of limited rhyme that set the pattern for the rhymed couplets and random rhyme scattered throughout the poem. The remaining stanzaic pattern of the poem roams from couplets and tercets to varying verse lengths, that accent Satin-Legs' free-wheeling lifestyle. Metrically, the poem most often hovers about iambic pentameter and delves into the particulars of Satin-Legs' life examining the sights, sounds, and scents of Bronzeville, weighing them against the material acquisitions of the dominant white society.

Having defined Satin-Legs by his ritualistic ruses, the narrator's satiric tone turns sardonic as she shifts her focus to the disdainful, silent, white observer and probes the plausibility of his humanistic intentions to improve upon Satin-Legs' world of stymied pretensions:

> Now, at his bath, would you deny him lavender
> Or take away the powcr of his pine?
> What smelly substitute, heady as wine,
> Would you provide? life must be aromatic. (42)

By focusing on a series of cultural contrasts, the narrator toys with the unrealistic options and alternatives of the "straight tradition" to which Satin-Legs might avail himself and that would meet with the approval of the elitist observer. The narrator skillfully manipulates a flower motif to suggest the wide disparity in Satin-Legs' and the observer's respective stations in life then queries the observer as to whether or not the more expensive varieties of fresh flowers such as "Asters? a Really Good geranium? / A white carnation?" would suit Satin-Legs' lifestyle. She reminds the observer that, for Satin-Legs, fresh flowers signify only the wild "dandelions" that grow randomly in the ghetto, or the decorative funeral rites associated with death.

Finally, the narrator pauses in her intensive dialogue to survey the landscape of Satin-Legs' lowly origins:

> But you forget, or did you ever know,
> His heritage of cabbage and pigtails,
> Old intimacy with alleys, garbage pails,
> Down in the deep (but always beautiful) South
> Where roses blush their blithest (it is said)
> And sweet magnolias put Chanel to shame. (43)

The narrator's emphatic "No!" to her own question and commentary upon Satin-Legs' poverty, in the land of plenty, fuels her continuing examination of the white observer's lack of a finite understanding of Satin-Legs' life as the archetypal poor, urban, Black man and the extent to which white society must venture to equalize things.[20]

Brooks forcefully empowers the narrator when she pointedly imposes parenthesis upon the dialogue to shift the burden of cultural assimilation, from Satin-Legs, to the privileged white society.[21] The narrator then ruminates over the question of material sacrifice as a methodology for balancing social inequality:

> Ah, there is little hope. You might as well—
> Unless you care to set the world a-boil
> And do a lot of equalizing things,
> Remove a little ermine, say, from kings,
> Shake hands with paupers and appoint them men,
> For instance—certainly you might as well
> Leave him his lotion, lavender and oil. (43)

As she proceeds to examine Satin-Legs' meager accouterments of wealth, the narrator enters into a brief conspiratorial alliance with the observer: "Let us proceed. Let us inspect, together / With his meticulous and serious love, / The innards of this closet. Which is a vault." The value of the narrator's sense of double-consciousness becomes apparent as she deftly peruses Satin-Legs' artistic creations and contrasts them with real material wealth.

Although his collection of prized possessions is bereft of "diamonds," "pearls," and "silver plate," Satin-Legs is rich in "wonder-suits," "Ballooning pants," and "hats / Like bright umbrellas and hysterical ties / Like narrow banners for some gathering war." But after tickling the poetic fancy of the observer by cataloging Satin-Legs' valuables in a tone of affectionate hyperbole, the astute narrator turns abruptly lyrical in a brief aside and suddenly declares that Satin-Legs' exuberant "zoot-suit" wardrobe is no real substitute for a life of economic deprivation and the "little coins" of poverty.[22] She bemoans his loss in a couplet that veers off sharply from the general tone of the poem, yet foreshadows its end:

> People are so in need, in need of help.
> People want so much that they do not know. (44)

With a dramatic jolt, the double-consciousness of the narrator fades momentarily; and from her privileged perch, she announces an emotional alliance with Satin-Legs and his community as she recalls the "Promise piled over and betrayed," an allusion informed by the Emancipation "promise" of "forty acres and a mule" for the freedmen to begin new and fruitful lives.[23]

Having established Satin-Legs in the narcissistic veneer of one who "loves himself," the narrator sweeps him from the illusions of his private rooms to the "smear" of poverty that awaits him below in the ghetto. As they embark upon an excursion of the cultural realities of Satin-Legs' racially segregated and economically deprived community, the narrator reminds the silent white observer that he has been privy to all the "sculpture and . . . art" that Satin-Legs possesses and states, "You forget and you forget."

As Satin-Legs embarks upon a familiar jaunt through the

streets of Bronzeville, he ignores the sounds and sights of poverty and filth:

> Out. Sounds about him smear,
> Become a unit. He hears and does not hear
> The alarm clock meddling in somebody's sleep;
> Children's governed Sunday happiness;
> The dry tone of a plane; a woman's oath;
> Consumption's spiritless expectoration;
> An indignant robin's resolute donation (45)

Likewise, he is protected by the "blurred" vision of his unconsciousness:

> He sees and does not see the broken windows
> Hiding their shame with newsprint; little girl
> With ribbons decking wornness, little boy
> Wearing the trousers with the decentest patch, (45)

Through the narrator's examination of the filth and disease, the dead spittle of tuberculosis, and the germs of bird droppings, even given the high rhetorical jargon of the speaker, it is clear that the health and vitality of the community are at stake as a result of the unsanitary conditions that persist.[24]

Against the backdrop of societal norms, as represented by the narrator and subtly attributable to the silent white observer, the stark message of Satin-Legs' life is illuminated in a solitary neon stanza:

> He loiters.

Brooks' choice of the word "loiters" strategically defines the urban Black man whose destiny is codified by a limited number of ghetto survival techniques—"Staying Alive," "Having a Good Time," "Praising God," "Getting Ahead," and "Advancing the Race"—that define the confining parameters of his aspirations (Drake 385). She exploits the traditional pastoral images of loitering, as exemplified in John Keats "La Belle Dame Sans Merci" where the "haggard, and so woebegone" knight sojourns in the plush recesses of nature to assuage his emotionally tormented soul, "Alone and palely loitering," to offer a negative connotation of loitering, vivid in the emancipated slaves who wandered aimlessly and were often accused of vagrancy as they scoured the land for new opportunities.[25] Satin-Legs lolls about the busy thoroughfare of Bronzeville, amid a wailing, moaning, and destitute populous, in search of a good time. In the urban setting, Brooks' use of "loiter" takes on a new and more racially charged meaning, which also informs later works like the pool players of "We Real Cool," who "lurk late," and "A Bronzeville Mother Loiters in Mississippi. Meanwhile, a Mississippi Mother Burns Bacon" (*The Bean Eaters*).

As Satin-Legs ambles amid the visible stagnation and deprivation of Bronzeville, the narrator drifts into a cultural reverie and explores both Satin-Legs' recent familial, as well as his more distant ancestral past. She holds out no hope for any lingering vestiges of memory on Satin-Legs' part that could define him as a conduit of history because in his lack of historical and cultural consciousness, "He quite considers his reactions his." Ultimately, the narrator's thoughtful musings distance her from the earlier cynical remarks directed at the silent white observer, and instead, more closely align her thinking with that of Satin-Legs. As Satin-Legs "loiters," the narrator is no longer "warring" with the duality of her own soul and in the cessation of that internal battle now sees Satin-Legs, not in contrast to white society, but, on his own terms—in the epitome of his identity.

While the street scenes surround Satin-Legs in a plague of poverty that is mirrored in the faces of ghetto men "familiar with the guiding awe / Of foodlessness," the "sore avenues" of Bronzeville are haunted by jukebox sounds as "Restaurant vendors / Weep, or out of them rolls a restless glee" called the blues:

> The Lonesome Blues, the Long-lost Blues, I Want A
> Big Fat Mama. Down these sore avenues
> Comes no Saint-Saëns, no piquant elusive Grieg,
> And not Tschaikovsky's wayward eloquence
> And not the shapely tender drift of Brahms.
> But could he love them?. . . (45)

The narrator suggests that the classical music of Europe is not the appropriate vessel to carry Satin-Legs' unconscious pain from "bits of forgotten hate. . . . [for] The little dream that his father humored: the thing / His sister did for money." Not only does the reference to classic blues lamentations define the suffering of the impoverished Black community, it also provides a stark societal contrast to the affluent flavor of the European society which does not touch Satin-Legs' world.[26]

Ralph Ellison captures the gripping pain of the blues in his statement:

> Their attraction lies in this, that they at once express both the agony of life and the possibility of conquering it through sheer toughness of spirit. They fall short of tragedy only in that they provide no solution, offer no scapegoat but the self. (104)

Although the blues do not profess to offer solutions to the woes they address, historically, the blues have been credited with providing an emotional release for wearied spirits and a soothing balm for the pent up grief of a ravaged and torn people. The blues offer a salve that temporarily relieves and revives the victimized then propels them forward for the next round of life's ongoing battle for survival.

Just as Sterling Brown's rural blues sing of both the natural disasters and racial injustices that confront the Southern

Black agrarians who vie with nature for survival, in poems like "Tornado Blues," "Children of the Mississippi," and "St. Louis Blues"; and Langston Hughes sings a migrated blues of Northern economic disparity and torn love relationships, in poems like "Sylvester's Dying Bed," "The Weary Blues," and "To Midnight Nan at Leroy's"; Brooks infuses the dramatic pathos of Satin-Legs' urban environment with the sorrowful strains of the blues.[27] As Sterling Brown states in "Blues, Ballads, and Social Songs," "the mood of the blues is deep melancholy in spite of some humor. But the humor is often wry, twisted, ironic" (18).

So lost is Satin-Legs in his Sunday dalliance that he misses the impact of the tarnished scene before him as the cause for urban blues, and in his blasé detachment, takes everything at its surface value. But, in a stanza that explains his historical blindness, the narrator constructs Satin-Legs' internalization of and resistance to a racial past haunted by slavery and oppression. Satin-Legs ignores the nudges of his "ancestors" who "Crowd him. Fog out his identity. . . . He quite considers his reactions his, / Judges he walks most powerfully alone, / That everything is—simply what it is." Satin-Legs' attention is so riveted on having a good time, even in the midst of squalor and poverty, that on a conscious level, he virtually escapes the flood of historic pain and ventures forth on his quest for mind-releasing forms of Sunday entertainment to placate the unconscious "grievous wounds" of the blues.[28]

Though submerged beneath the surface of his reality, an aspect of Satin-Legs' racial plight is revealed in his pleasurable Sunday jaunt to the movie theater. When Satin-Legs views a romantic movie with a white hero and heroine, he understands the subtle racial innuendos of the movie and thus subverts his real racial hostilities. It is "time to boo / The hero's kiss, and boo the heroine / Whose ivory and yellow it is sin / For his eye to eat of." The negative reaction displayed by this Black man is a spontaneous response to America's obsession with race and sex and its history of lynching Black men who openly or purportedly display admiration for white women. Thus Satin-Legs' reaction is automatic, almost programmed, in a world where racial taboos unadhered to can mean death.[29] The movie is a blatant reminder of his outsidedness in a society that baits Black men with the forbidden fruit of white womanhood. By contrast, he displays affection for the Mickey Mouse cartoon character who "is for everyone in the house" (46).

The subtle edge of social protest in the poem becomes more apparent as the narrator's veil of double-consciousness slips discreetly away, and she distances herself from the silent white observer. In the final verses of the poem, the narrator's consciousness merges with that of Satin-Legs and finally affords her the visual acuity to see him on his own terms. Satin-Legs makes no pretensions about his life, but simply strives to survive independently. Although R. Baxter Miller states that "Satin-legs fails, not because of an unwillingness to confront a naturalistic world but in the ignorance which keeps him from defining the world" (102), Satin-Legs actually succeeds by surviving, in spite of the odds, in a society that provides him no succor, but willfully limits his aspirations by limiting his opportunities in its "daily and dramatic rejection" of him (*Metropolis* xxx).

Metaphorically, Richard Wright offers a lucid definition that illuminates the outcome of the oppressive social processes which duly restrict Black life in Bronzeville: "The imposed conditions under which Negroes live detail the structure of their lives like an engineer outlining the blue-prints for the production of machines" (*Metropolis* xx). In an analysis of Bronzeville's "imposed Black Belt existence," composed of Negroes who are "completely socially excluded," Wright lends his voice of social clarity when he poses a question:

What peculiar personality formations result when millions of

> people are forced to live lives of outward submissiveness while trying to keep intact in their hearts a sense of the worth of their humanity? What are the personality mechanisms that sublimate racial resentments which, if expressed openly, would carry penalties varying from mild censure to death? (*Metropolis* xxx)

Satin-Legs' makeshift rituals for survival enable him to create an agenda that carries his signature. Just as Sterling Brown creatively depicts "Sporting Beasly" and "Slim Greer," Langston Hughes offers "Jesse B. Semple," and Margaret Walker contributes "Poppa Chicken," Brooks too creates a memorable character who succeeds, not according to traditional societal norms, but against the grain and by his own definition.

As the narrator trails Satin-Legs into the grand finale of his day, her view of him is no longer muddled by the veil of double-consciousness. She finally sees Satin through the sensory tripod of his self-defined world and reports his pursuit of physical gratification without intruding upon the narrative to explain or exonerate him from his choices and actions for the benefit of the silent white observer. The narrator has finally freed herself sufficiently to permit Satin-Legs to tell his own story by way of his actions, and in doing so, shocks both herself and the reader when Satin-Legs, in his own lyrical voice, sensually strokes the reader's sensibilities in the final stanza.

In a stanza that opens with a note of bathos, the narrator reports that Satin-Legs "Squires his lady to dinner at Joe's Eats." But the touch of the cavalier initially implied is easily dispelled as the photograph of Satin's date is enlarged by the narrator. From that portrait emerges a "lady" who, in her exaggerated countenance, is the female counterpart of Satin-Legs:

> In Queen Lace stockings with ambitious heels
> That strain to kiss the calves, and vivid shoes
> Frontless and backless, Chinese fingernails,

> Earrings, three layers of lipstick, intense hat
> Dripping with the most voluble of veils. (46, 47)

The power of the poem manifests itself as the newly positioned narrator accepts Satin-Legs in all of his self-stylized costumery and embellishments. In her final word to the now distant observer, she cautions that no further comparisons be made of Satin-Legs' lifestyle and his choices: because Satin-Legs is not well-versed in the "quiet arts of compromise. He would / Not understand your counsels on control, nor / Thank you for your late trouble."

Satin-Legs and his lady dine sufficiently at a local eatery that replicates other Bronzeville soul food kitchens like Ernie's Kitchen Shack, the Avenue Lounge, the Original Fish Shop, the DuSable Lounge and Bar, and the "exclusive 'Eat Shoppe'" defined in Drake and Cayton's *Black Metropolis*, where both local dignitaries and common folk meet to enjoy the common fare (380).

> At Joe's Eats
> You get your fish or chicken on meat platters.
> With coleslaw, macaroni, candied sweets,
> Coffee and apple pie. You go out full.
> (The end is—isn't it?—all that really matters.) (47)

In the final segment of the poem, it is clear that the narrator understands and thus impresses upon the reader the raw physicality of Satin-Legs' life that demands the same gratification as his recently abated desire for entertainment and food. Satin-Legs' specificity in his choices of film, food, and women leaves no doubt as to the caliber of his interests; his taste in women sits in sharp contrast to Brooks' portrait of the young woman in "obituary for a living lady," who refuses even "a touch of the best cream / cologne" and goes "without lipstick" (34). His inclinations are more closely aligned to the imagery created by the young girl of "a song in the front yard" whose life holds little adventure. Unlike her mother who views the neighborhood woman "Johnny Mae," as "bad," the young girl sings: "And I'd like to be a bad woman, too, / And wear the brave stockings of night-black lace / And strut down the streets with paint on my face" (28).

When Satin-Legs emerges as poet in the lyric epilogue of the poem, the sensual quality of his voice is surprisingly tender, an ironic contrast to a character profile that renders him shallow by comparison to Euro-American representations. His language is distinctly reminiscent of Jean Toomer's "Karintha," where the narrator chants: "Her skin is like dusk on the eastern horizon." In analogous tones, the fertile imagery of Satin-Legs' fantasy life unfolds when he evinces a whimsical beauty, like the whisper of love words rustling through Southern pine trees, and savors the true beauty of his Northern ghetto life:

> *Her body is like new brown bread*
> *Under the Woolworth mignonette.*
> *Her body is a honey bowl*
> *Whose waiting honey is deep and hot.*
> *Her body is like summer earth,*
> *Receptive, soft, and absolute . . .* (Brooks' italics, 47)

Kent is right on target when he states that "The Sundays of Satin-Legs Smith" is the "power poem" of *A Street in Bronzeville.* Brooks wields her poetic quill expertly to depict a ghetto character whose definition of his life suggests beauty on his own terms; it is what Kent calls "the indomitability of the human spirit in its quest for beauty" (69). "Satin-Legs' triumph" is his ability to survive in a society that is not predisposed to include him in its social equality; instead, he is bound in Bronzeville's "forgotten jungle of black life" (Wright xxxi). Thus, it is his own act of self-creation that will continue to sustain him. Satin-Legs' ghetto stance might well have informed Nikki Giovanni's first-person narrator in "Nikki-Rosa" who tells the reader about the negative media perceptions of her ghetto life but insists: "all the while I was quite happy."

Brooks' success in "The Sundays of Satin-Legs Smith" is her skillful portrayal of a character who can evoke both awe and pity in the reader by his ability to circumvent dismal failure in a society that offers him little hope of successful survival. Yet, Satin-Legs does survive and thrive in his world with a make-do-ness that sits in sharp contrast to the Euro-American value system profiled by the "double-consciousness" of the sophisticated narrator. Despite the obstacles produced by a racist America—residential segregation, rampant discrimination, economic deprivation, and social inequality—Satin-Legs, in the epitome of his identity, is proof-positive that Black Americans can survive even in the oppression of America's Bronzevilles.

There is no question that Brooks' poetic voice is a chime that consistently rings the bell of inequality and announces the limitations placed on Black life in a racist society. Likewise, her canvas of Black life in America depicts the oppressive conditions nurtured to full growth in the soil of racial discrimination, residential segregation, economic exploitation, and social inequality. Yet Brooks extends her poetic efforts beyond the parameters of the urban community to examine the persistent racial "fences" that defy the Black patriots' contributions to America's military might, patriots who split their energies to fight an ironic war against the racist ideologies of foreign powers while battling for racial equality at home.

In "Negro Hero" and the "Gay Chaps At The Bar" sonnet series Brooks struggles to depict the dilemmas confronting Black soldiers of World War II who faced forward to fight a war against racist ideologies abroad, yet who intermittently and anxiously turned backward toward domestic shores to assess the ongoing battle for racial equality at home. In *From Slavery to Freedom*, John Hope Franklin examines the domestic battlefield where Black men fought stridently for democracy versus discrimination in their efforts to become full and equal citizens. Of the three million Black men and women who answered the enlistment call, approximately one million were admitted to the armed forces, only to serve in the most menial jobs (Franklin 390). In his appraisal *Blacks in America's Wars*, Robert W. Mullen acknowledges the "Double V" attitude that persisted among Black servicemen in World War II and affirms that: "it was only natural that Blacks should feel that they were involved in two simultaneous wars—one against Hitler in Germany, and the other against the Hitlers in the United States" (Mullen 54). The sheer hypocrisy involved in establishing segregated military units to fight an enemy with a more overt "master-race ideology" is the theme of Brooks' war poetry (55).

Brooks establishes a first-person narrative perspective to accommodate the voices of Black soldiers who tell riveting stories of the psychologically injurious nature of war as a reflection of America's racist politics that blur the distinctions between foreign and domestic enemies. In "Dialectics of Desire," Ann Folwell Stanford adroitly notes that these poems address the "tenuous and contradictory situation of black soldiers in a white man's army . . . by making the direct link between war and racism, thus narrowing the gap between military (foreign) and racial (American) struggle, between soldiers and civilians" (197). In these war poems, Brooks' tone of social commentary is stark as she redefines "war" from the perspective of Black soldiers who must fight a dubious battle abroad to insure the rights of others, while simultaneously waging a fierce fight at home to secure the "Four Freedoms," ostensibly granted to them by the American creed.

Brooks infiltrates the male domain of war poetry by establishing the active male persona of a soldier on the front, the force of which rings out in the voice of a soldier at war.[30] "Negro

Hero / to suggest Dorie Miller" lauds the military accomplishments of an actual Black naval mess attendant, second class, who was assigned to menial labor, not combat, aboard the battleship USS *West Virginia*, during the Pearl Harbor attack. Following an attack by the Japanese, Miller saved the ship and his comrades, by successfully attacking four Japanese bomber planes.

In a dramatic monologue, the narrator speaks between the clenched teeth of controlled rage, citing the paradox of patriotism and prejudice in America. In the opening stanza, he insistently pursues his belief that he should "save" America's obstinate, "drowning men" from a willful death:

> I had to kick their law into their teeth in order to save
> them.
> However I have heard that sometimes you have to deal
> Devilishly with drowning men in order to swim them to
> shore. (48)

From his self-convincing posture, the speaker relives his brief basking in the sun and the "glory" he earned as a reward for his rescue efforts; he states: "For I am a gem." Doubtless he had to save the ship, both for his own survival and the survival of his shipmates, even though he was not deemed sufficiently worthy for training in combat techniques. Ironically, his suggestion that while crucifixion, or death by "spikes in the afterward hands," would have been his punishment for failure, had he not "put gold on their / name," equality, or full life, is not the reward for his success. Parentheses point to the consideration of what he deems a major issue, yet recognizes is only an aside for his compatriots: "(They are not concerned that it was hardly The Enemy / my fight was against / But them.)."

Yet, even in the face of that reality, his pride pulses rapidly in the face of his accolades, and he admits: "I was wild." Held fast by the thrill of combat, he recalls his boyhood dreams of battle, which had been all but snuffed out by his restricted duties aboard ship:

> It was a tall time. And of course my blood was
> Boiling about in my head and straining and howling
> and singing me on.
> Of course I was rolled on wheels of my boy itch to get
> at the gun.
> Of course all the delicate rehearsal shots of my child-
> hood massed in mirage before me. (48)

Though he wallows in the warmth of national heroism, the speaker's feet hit the ground with the resounding smack of reality when he admits that democracy does not love him with an equal degree of reciprocity. He acknowledges that "Their white-gowned democracy was my fair lady. / With her knife lying cold, straight, in the softness of / her sweet-flowing sleeve." And, in a tone of an increasingly studied agitation, the hero asks, "am I good enough to die for them . . . Or do I intrude even now?" He struggles to control his seething anger as he wonders, "is my place while death licks his lips and / strides to them / In the galley still?" Finally, the hero understands that his act of heroism has changed nothing.

As he attempts to salvage some sliver of pride, the hero recalls the Southern white man who said, "I'd rather be dead . . . Than saved by the drop of a black man's blood." In the final stanza, the speaker finally awakens to the creeping awareness that his efforts were in vain. Although he feeds himself a sense of false assurance when he states, "Naturally, the important thing is, I helped to save them, / them and a part of their democracy," he is faced with the final grim reality of America's stance on race relations. His latent suspicions of an unspoken creed of inequality for Blacks bursts into glorious flower, as his pride in a job well done wilts in the face of continued discrimination. He is content:

> Despite this possible horror: that they might prefer the
> Preservation of their law in all its sick dignity and their
> knives
> To the continuation of their creed
> And their lives. (50)

Enlarging upon the theme of "Negro Hero," two final poems from *A Street in Bronzeville* originate in the "Gay Chaps At The Bar" series and are infused with social commentary. Although the entire series of war sonnets underscores the complex emotional and psychological ramifications of war, the sonnets, "the white troops had their orders but the Negroes looked like men" and "the progress" send the most stark messages of protest to address the racism in America's armed forces. The sonnet form, in its often rigid adherence to the static formulas which mirror the distinct restrictions defining both the Petrarchan and Shakespearean models, is the perfect vessel to transport the implications of form and order inherent to military ideology. By its very definition of lyricism in the traditional classical usage, the sonnet has the capacity to deliver the pathos of Black soldiers struggling with American racism, while paradoxically, because it signifies the highest form of poetic art, elevating a subject that degrades the American creed by equating it with a revered poetic form.

Early on, Gladys Margaret Williams notes in "Gwendolyn Brooks' Way with the Sonnet," Brooks learned from the Harlem classicists, James Weldon Johnson, Langston Hughes, and Sterling Brown, "that the folk forms could be made to bend, yet not break, could be as richly complex as any sonnet" (216). In addition to gaining poetic expertise in the folk forms, Brooks had tackled European forms of poetry, such as the sonnet, with fierce success. Thus Brooks' mastery of a form which carries the signatures of Shakespeare, Spenser, Milton, Donne, Keats, and Wordsworth, yet one which she individualized by her own affinity with the modernistic tenets of Pound, Eliot, Yeats, and Frost, has produced a display of incredible adroitness in dispensing with strict poetic patterns.

In the Petrarchan sonnet, "the white troops had their orders but the Negroes looked like men," the third-person speaker uses the octave to establish a dichotomy of images that differentiate between society's stereotypical character profiles of the white and the Negro soldiers.

> They had supposed their formula was fixed.
> They had obeyed instructions to devise
> A type of cold, a type of hooded gaze.
> But when the Negroes came they were perplexed.
> These Negroes looked like men . . . (70)

In its allusion to white soldiers, the tone of the opening line is coolly martial as it invokes the tight formations of the military in the alliteration of "formula was fixed." But as Williams' vernacular phrasing so aptly suggests, "Things shake loose when the Negroes come" (225). What follows the revelation that the historical stereotypes of Negroes have been artificially manufactured is an instant dismantling of the stereotypical racial views that have held the white soldiers hostage and a willful relaxation of military burial laws. Thus, the men dispense with the rigorous assignment of bodies by racial distinctions: "A box for dark men and a box for Other—" and care little that the bodies would be "scrambled" mistakenly or "switched" intentionally in coffins. The theme of their new cognizance is: "Who really gave two figs?" Their awakening to the sameness of men, even in the face of racial difference, drives them to the broad pronouncements evident in the closing lines:

> Neither the earth nor heaven ever trembled.
> And there was nothing startling in the weather. (70)

If there is any indication of hope in the face of the vigorous protest of Brooks' war sonnets, it is in the suggestion that by coming together in the military, Black men and white men can see for themselves, beyond the stereotypical turf of racism, that men are men, regardless of color. It is in this vein that "the progress" proposes questions of patriotism. The collective "we" of the poem anxiously examines American patriotism, only to uncover the nagging doubt that it may not be evenly distributed. The poem begs the question of any real racial "progress" in America. In the opening line, the speaker sets the stage for his concerns as a continuation of a tragic revelation:

> And still we wear our uniforms, follow
> The cracked cry of the bugles, comb and brush
> Our pride and prejudice, doctor the sallow
> Initial ardor, wish to keep it fresh.
> Still we applaud the President's voice and face.
> Still we remark on patriotism, sing,
> Salute the flag, thrill heavily, rejoice
> For death of men who too saluted, sang. (75)

With the opening "But" of the sestet, the speaker counters the surface appearance of patriotism to the reality of "A fear, a deepening hollow through the cold." He questions the ability of soldiers to resume blind normalcy when he asks, "even if we come out standing up / How shall we smile, congratulate. . . ?" Thus, the reality of racism, and the minor appearance of progress have indeed changed the soldiers' perceptions of America. Akin to the speaker in "Negro Hero," this speaker's awakening is a painful one and leaves him no real recourse to mend his deluded allegiance. Instead, he resumes his military posture and orders: "Listen, listen. The step / Of iron feet again. And again wild."

In *A Street In Bronzeville,* Brooks' voice of social protest is often subtle and sometimes snared in the apparatus of poetic form, yet she consistently conveys the oppressive plight of her community in strategic poems like "kitchenette building," "the mother," "the ballad of chocolate Mabbie," "of De Witt Williams on his way to Lincoln Cemetery," "The Sundays of Satin-Legs Smith," "Negro Hero," "Hattie Scott," "Queen of the Blues," and "Gay Chaps At The Bar." Brooks balances these poems that define her social vision with the character vignettes that serve as photographs of those who people her community. Through the form of her ballads, blues, and sonnets, she paints an authentic picture of Bronzeville, in the expressive content of all its hopes, pains, and realities. Through her poetry, Brooks creates a blueprint of America's Black metropolis that defines the Black American urban ghetto where people strive to survive. Brooks, gently and provocatively, probes and protests the vise of economic exploitation held firmly in place by the screws of American racism.

Chapter III

The 1940s: A Milieu for Integrationist Poetics

Gwendolyn Brooks, like many women poets, often wrote under challenging, and sometimes adverse conditions, considering the oppositional demands of artistry and domesticity. Given that as a point of discussion, *Annie Allen* raises certain questions.[1] Why did Brooks opt to approach the story of women—motherhood, daughterhood, womanhood—from such a complex technical perspective? Who constructed the artistic proving ground that demanded such a grueling exercise in prosody, language, and imagery? What were the rewards? What, in essence, were the conditions, social and literary, contributing to her need to create a framework of a classical mock-epic as the vessel for a colloquial tale?

The social and literary climate of Brooks' second book of poetry, *Annie Allen* (1949), was strategically impacted by the new spirit of optimism emanating from the postwar period of the 1940s. In "New Poets," Margaret Walker gives a brief but succinct overview of the historical setting in which Black writers came to "unusual prominence as poets" (345). The strong note of social protest, brought about by racial oppression and war, was especially evident in the poetry published between 1935 and 1945: Brooks' *A Street in Bronzeville* (1945), Robert Hayden's *Heart-Shape in the Dust* (1940), Margaret Walker's *For My People* (1942), and Melvin Tolson's *Rendezvous with America* (1944).[2] But as the social and economic status of Black Americans reflected some small measure of the prosperity generated by the New Deal and World War II, protest poetry began to level off in the late 1940s as a reflection of that optimism (Walker 348).

In an interview with Ida Lewis, Brooks comments on how she viewed the Black world in the 1940s and 50s: "I thought that integration was the solution. All we had to do was keep on appealing to the whites to help us, and they would" (*RPO* 175). Likewise, there was no question in her mind as to the identity of the target audience for her poetry: "It was whites who were reading and listening to us" (*RPO* 176). The "us" Brooks refers to in a 1940s context would have included her literary peers, Hayden, Walker, and Tolson. In her essay, "Poets Who are Negroes," Brooks clarifies the literary gauntlet that had been thrust in front of the Black writer:

> no real artist is going to be content with offering raw materials. The Negro poet's most urgent duty, at present, is to polish his technique, his way of presenting his truths and his beauties, that these may be more insinuating, and therefore, more overwhelming. (312)

A. P. Davis examines the period of transition in America that informed the works of Black writers in the 1940s in his essay "Integration and Race Literature." The "spiritual climate" of the country was pro-integration, and early attempts were visible in the armed forces, Southern graduate and professional educational institutions, and in extended voting rights (607). Davis notes that in the days of rampant discrimination and segregation, the 1920s and 30s, Black writers, fueled by the hostile efforts of their "common enemy" to resist all efforts at integration, "capitalized on oppression" in their creative endeavors of the 1940s (607). In *Black Writers of America*, Richard Barksdale and Keneth Kinnamon identify "the Black writer's need to write out of the context of the Black experience," and note that "Richard Wright's experience as a Black creative artist in America revealed that Black literary expression was inextricably linked to Black political, social, and economic experience" (654). The new mood of integration, while still controversial in many quarters of American life, gained a sufficient foothold, sending writers who had previously relied on the voice of protest in their literature to search for new thematic and aesthetic ground.[3]

Following the example of Harvard scholar Alain Locke, who provided critical direction to the writers of the Harlem Renaissance, a fresh school of Black scholars surfaced in the 1940s and 50s to formulate new critical theories, quite at variance with the old ones.[4] Barksdale and Kinnamon perceptively assert that based upon their training in Southern Black colleges, these energetic and articulate young critics used "objective precision," as opposed to the "hortatory eloquence" of Locke in the formulation of their critical opinions and undauntingly "applied the critical standards of the white literary establishment" (654). The "incisive criticism" of these literary "mainstreamers," especially J. Saunders Redding, Hugh Gloster, and Nick Aaron Ford, was a definitive statement of their contention that the goal of the Black writer should be "full integration into the mainstream of American life" (655).

In his essay, "Race and the Negro Writer," Gloster affirms his position as a staunch idealist for integration by outlining the ways in which an effusive use of "racial subject matter has handicapped the Negro writer" (369). He sees the Black writer as falling literary prey to the menace of "certain critics and publishers" who would "lure him into the deadly trap of cultural segregation by advising him that the Black ghetto is his proper milieu and that he will write best when he is most Negroid" (369). For Gloster, the alternative is a "gradual emancipation . . . from the fetters of racial chauvinism and cultural isolation" made possible by what he sees as a climate of democracy in America's literary melting pot (370).

Gloster offers an optimistic prognosis for Black writers to assimilate into mainstream white society by correcting the negative trend of culturally segregated writing that he feels has sorely "retarded" their artistic growth. He suggests that Black writers strive to lift their work to the "universal plane" by transcending the color line as Wright did in *Native Son* and create a literature that celebrates "all mankind" (370).[5] In his quest to nudge the Black writer from a posture of "ethnic individuality" to his own lofty ideal of a "universal point of view" (371), Gloster closes his essay with the bugle call of patriotism for the Black writer to become an American writer:

> The Negro writer is also an American writer, a man of letters as free as any of his national confreres to tap the rich literary resources of our land and its people. To accept the principle that racial experience is the only natural province of the Negro writer is to approve an artistic double standard that is just as confining and demoralizing in American literature as is segregation in American life. (371)

Gloster's critical posture favoring integration was not unusual at a time when Black writers hoped that America would become a united nation, rather than remain a divided one. In the same issue of *Phylon*, J. Saunders Redding, in the densely worded, but optimistic essay, "The Negro Writer—Shadow and Substance," shares a vision of hope for integration and encouraged Black writers to take advantage of "the social and intellectual and spiritual climate of Roosevelt's New Deal and of the world's second war," as an impetus for a change in outlook (372). Like Gloster, Redding earmarks a universality in writing about the human—not the Black—condition, yet asserts that the highest goal a Black writer can attain is an obscure "realistic idealism and a sort of scientific humanism" (372). Oddly, though Redding calls for Black writers to liberate themselves from their "racial chains" because they are "in no fundamental way different and particular," conversely, he ends his essay with a call to them to observe their "special category of race-experience" to uncover "a mine of creative material" (373).

Nick Aaron Ford issued the most balanced and polished statement on the debate, in direct refutation of the pure integrationist theories posited by Gloster and Redding. Different in tone and perspective, Ford's essay, "A Blueprint for Negro Authors," is stark in its simplicity: "despite one hundred and ninety years of effort, no American Negro poet has achieved a status comparable to such first-rate poets as Robert Frost or Edwin Arlington Robinson" (374). Having first issued the explicit challenge of achieving technical excellence in literature, Ford offers the "harassed author" clearly enumerated guidelines to attain a "master of craftsmanship" (374). Ford's basic premise is that although Black artists must not be compelled to forfeit their racial consciousness, they must subordinate any tendency to usurp art with pure propaganda. But, rather than displaying unqualified support for the tenet of "art for art's sake," Ford requires that social propaganda, as indicative of the time, not be ignored, but skillfully woven into the fabric of artistic patterns, as a "legitimate ingredient of serious literature" (376).

The weakness of Ford's essay is that, though he draws attention to the dearth of excellence in Black poetry, his real interest, or perhaps expertise, is situated in the technical aspects of fiction writing for examples of what he views as "chief weaknesses . . . in the area of craftsmanship and design" (374). Yet his crucial point is crystal clear; Black writers, both poets and fiction writers, must excel in the quest for technical proficiency by cloaking the ever-present message of social commentary within the folds of craftsmanship. Ford's primary criteria for alleviating what he views as an artistic deficiency are the creative characterization, inventiveness of conversation, and construction of setting and mood apparent in the fictional works of Richard Wright and Willard Motley, without forfeiting cultural nuances and racial themes.[6]

In a tone of subtlely veiled sarcasm, Ford brusquely dismisses the notion that Black writers should avoid racial themes and material, "and leave to white authors the exploitation of subject matter dealing with Negro life" (375). To challenge that view, he suggests: "I cannot believe that a Negro, sensitive, as all artists must be, can feel and understand anything in America as minutely and as truthfully as he can the effects of race" (375). But the reality of the influence of integration efforts facing the conscious artist was clear; as A. P. Davis writes in his essay: "protest writing has become the first casualty of the new racial climate" (608). Black fiction writers like Zora Neale Hurston, Richard Wright, Ann Petry, and Chester Himes, who had successfully published early works out of a clear racial milieu, dutifully responded to the literary dictum to elevate their works to a universal plane, representing the essence of all humanity, by issuing later works that were clearly explorations in white themes and characterizations.[7] These "universal" works did not receive the critical acclaim alluded to by the new school of critical forecasters, nor did they move the redefined Black writers into the full status of white Americans. Instead, much of the literature, focusing on the obstacles common to all humanity, died a quiet death of literary exclusion.

Despite Ford's oversight in the poetic genre, the literary and critical mandate he established for Black fiction writers, albeit unwittingly, reached the ears of the poets, whose artistic response was to create poetry with a global perspective. The tone of racial indignation that clings to Hayden's *Heart-Shape in the Dust* (1940), in poems like "Gabriel (Hanged for leading a slaved-revolt)" and "We Are the Hunted," was dramatically altered in the ornate diction and lavish imagery of lines from "A Ballad of Remembrance": "the sallow / vendeuse / of prepared tarnishes and jokes of nacre and / ormolu," as testament to his growing poetic maturity and freedom from racial mandates by the time he published *The Lion and the Archer* (1948). Tolson moved from the jarring protest of poems like "Rendezvous with

America" and "Dark Symphony" in *Rendezvous with America* (1944), to a sophisticated metrical diversity in his ode, *Libretto for the Republic of Liberia* (1953) that subverted and neutralized his tone of protest. Likewise, Gwendolyn Brooks made a radical departure from the overt focus on the poverty and oppression gripping the lives of Black people in *A Street in Bronzeville* (1945) to a heightened metrical sophistication, an experimental approach to language, and an allusive use of imagery that camouflaged her social commentary about the lives of Black women in *Annie Allen* (1949).

The literary explorations of Brooks, Hayden, and Tolson support the contention that Black writers did strive to manipulate their poetics into an acceptable mode that would be well-received by their white literary peers and audiences. The efforts of Black writers to join the white literary mainstream is evidenced by the words of Davis: "In an all-out effort to make integration become a reality, the Negro writer will tend to play down the remaining harshness in Negro American living and to emphasize the progress towards equality" (611). And in a failed prophecy, Redding's vision of assimilation of the Black writer by white culture signals the ultimate hope of integration: "the Black writer had found a white audience."[8] Although later found to be in err, the Zeitgeist of the time supported the general critical consensus that Black writers could actually assimilate into American literary life with no remaining traces of their distinctive cultural identity. But Barksdale and Kinnamon counter the optimistic perception of America's integrationist practices: "For, in the 1940s, despite the legal gains made on all fronts to win hitherto withheld political and social rights, America was still, literarily speaking, almost entirely lily-white" (654).

That Black writers not only heard the bell toll for proposed integration in America, but responded to its inviting ring, is evident and worthy of examination in the technical expertise exhibited in the subsequent works of Hayden, Tolson, and Brooks. Similarly, each of the poets wielded the razor-sharp points of his or her poetic quill to carve a distinctive niche in the white mainstream poetics of America. Though immediately responding to the ongoing critical dictate to assimilate into the mainstream of Western cultural tradition, the noted poets, in varying degrees, were also struggling against the vise of concrete racial definitions that had long threatened artistic individuality.[9]

Hayden, especially, swam against the tide of rhetoric directed at the question of racial identification, related to whether or not a Black artist must be labeled a "Black poet," as illuminated in Langston Hughes' 1926 essay, "The Negro Artist and the Racial Mountain." Hughes saw a growing tendency for white indoctrination in the artistic expressions of Black poets and confronted it by challenging them to define themselves by the richness of their own cultural heritage: "We younger Negro artists who create now intend to express our individual dark-skinned selves without fear or shame" (180). He attempted to combat a growing "urge toward whiteness" and "an aping of things white" in some Black artists by offering his own self-definition of being a "Black poet" who used the nuances of Black life as inspirations for writing:

> Most of my own poems are racial in theme and treatment, derived from the life I know. . . . So I am ashamed for the black poet who says, 'I want to be a poet, not a Negro poet,' as though his own racial world were not as interesting as any other world. (180)

Paradoxically, while the reality of the anthology Hayden edited, *Kaleidoscope: An Anthology of Negro Poets* (1967), admits to a need for an identifiable collection of Black literature "shaped over three centuries by social, moral, and literary forces essentially American," in its introduction, Hayden argues against such racial classifications. His resistance to being labeled a "Negro poet," as polar opposite to Hughes, is clear in his statement:

> But the effect of such labeling is to place any Negro author in a kind of literary ghetto where the standards applied to him, since he, being a 'spokesman for his race,' is not considered primarily a writer but a species of race-relations man, the leader of a cause, the voice of protest. (xx)[10]

The pressures of a social climate fueled by the dual and often conflicting demands of artistic autonomy and race consciousness facing Brooks, Hayden, and Tolson in the integration age of the 1940s nearly mirror those of the Harlem Renaissance poets Hughes, Claude McKay, and Countee Cullen. And in the 1940s, Hayden's struggle for racial and artistic autonomy mimicked the racial ambivalence of Cullen.[11] Where Brooks and Tolson also faced the dictate to write universally in language that could speak to all humanity, while proving that they could attain the same level of craftsmanship of the Modernist school, neither of them grappled with the issue of racial identification that was to be a lifelong battleground for Hayden.[12] In an interview with John O'Brien, Hayden vehemently argued his case against "strict definitions of what a poet is or should be" and instead, insisted that the poet forge his own artistic path maintaining the integrity and artistic freedom he felt was due him as an artist (115). Even given his mandate for recognition free of racial labeling, Hayden wrote an exquisitely textured poetics that celebrated the history of stoicism in Black Americans who conquered the life-threatening odds of slavery time and time again. The finely chiseled voice in the accentual sonnet "Frederick Douglass," the renegade rhythms of a slave escape in "Runagate Runagate," and the catharsis of blues rhythms in his tribute to blueswoman Bessie Smith, in "Homage to the Empress of the

Blues," tell of Hayden's intimate connection to Black life, if not to cultural self-identification.

Unlike Hayden, the pro-integrationist demand for a muted cultural identity left Tolson unperturbed; Tolson had no qualms about being called a "Negro poet," and at a conference of Black writers proudly announced: "I'm a black poet, an African-American poet, a Negro poet. I'm no accident—and I don't give a tinker's damn what you think."[13] Tolson developed his own literary armor for fighting the contention that Negro poets could not master white literary forms, yet must conquer those forms to be invited into mainstream America. Turning his attention from the struggle with racial identification to the proving ground of poetic excellence, he produced a poetics born of a cosmopolitan imagination, an ironic sense of humor, and a linguistic versatility.

In *Melvin B. Tolson*, Joy Flasch discusses the complexity of Tolson's work and the miniscule critical attention he received, like Hayden and Brooks, for poetry that defies easy explications (Flasch ii). Although Tolson had written three books by the 1940s, his second, *Libretto for the Republic of Liberia* written in 1947, was initially rejected by publishers and did not gain publication until 1953 (74). The work for which he is best known, *Harlem Gallery: Book I, The Curator*, was originally written in 1932, but was also rejected by publishers until its 1965 publication (ii). As testimony to the acknowledged stature of Tolson's work, he was able to engage eminent critics to write the introductions, but ultimately, it was that same influential status of the critics writing the introductions, not Tolson's poetry, that became his early calling card of literary acceptability (74, 134).

In 1947, Tolson was commissioned to write the *Libretto for the Republic of Liberia*, in celebration of the centennial of the founding of that African Republic. In the preface, critic Allen Tate effectively unlocked the door to white literary circles when he approved Tolson's "rich and complex language" by writing, "for the first time . . . a Negro poet has assimilated completely the full poetic language of his time and, by implication, the language of the Anglo-American poetic tradition" (ii). Though Tate, an influential leader of the New Poetry party, initially refused Tolson's request that he write the preface on the grounds of a too propagandistic tone in the book, he eventually complied when Tolson revised the eight-part poem by substituting the musical symbols of the diatonic scale and a broad scope of literary and historical allusions to assuage the offensive tone of propaganda and rescue his creation from the "provincial mediocrity" that Tate applied to the works of other Negro poets (Flasch 74). In lines from "RE," symptomatic of the extraordinary breadth of historic, classic, and poetic knowledge Tolson exhibited in the entire ode, Tolson had proven his artistic worth: "Europe bartered Africa crucifixes for red ivory, / Gewgaws for black pearls, *pierres d' aigris* for green gold" (Lines 68–9).

Similarly, critic Karl Shapiro established lifetime criteria for critical sparring with the mixed assessment that Tolson's *Harlem Gallery* was a "gift of tongues," "a work so fantastically stylized," with a "baroque surface," and topped off that critique with the definitive statement of Modernist obscurity: "Tolson writes and thinks in Negro" (12). Although lines from the opening segment of "ALPHA," "The Harlem Gallery, an Afric pepper bird, / awakes me at a people's dusk of dawn," and later references to *The Lord of the Flies*, "Byzantine" paintings, and "Tintoretto's *Paradise*," decry Shapiro's easy generalization, the major challenge to his statement is that in style, Tolson is akin to the school of Modernist poets, but in content, quite different. Tolson's use of metaphors, symbols, and juxtaposed ideas are similar to Eliot's work, but at that juncture, Tolson veers off into a different milieu. His work is derived from the Black community and is a celebration of its blackness; yet the Black community is not the audience to whom Tolson's work is directed, nor is it predominantly their language he is using. Flasch succinctly defines *Harlem Gallery* as "sociological commentary, an intellectual triple somersault" with the "vast mosaic" of Tolson's exaggerated use of mythological illusions, imagery from European literature and art, and extreme word-play, suggesting a lure for a white scholarly audience (99).[14]

The vibrations from the literary testing ground of the 1940s shook the early works of both Hayden and Tolson, yet altered their approaches to poetry in significantly different ways. Hayden was impelled by his natural affinity for historical research to absorb himself in a meticulous and scholarly study of Black history that enabled him to approach his poetic craft from an engrossing and contemplative stance. The result is an unrelenting collage of poetic voices that whisper the brutalities of Black history in the secure wrappings of technical expertise, expressive language, and historical grounding. Tolson's subsequent works reflect his incredible intellectual spunk, penchant for syntactical inversions, and subversive use of linguistic hyperbole to encompass his continuing but opaque message of social protest.

And finally, the same call for poetic craftsmanship over social commentary that was met by her Black literary peers, Hayden and Tolson, as an impetus for integration, was also heard by Brooks. She embarked upon a quest for new experimental ways of writing that would satisfy dual objectives. First, Brooks sought a poetics that would engage both Black and white critics, win acceptance from her white audience, and earn for her the reward of a secure position in the white mainstream school of arts and letters. Second, she needed to use her own source of inspiration, ordinary life around her, to tell her own poetic story. Brooks succeeded in her dual objectives. She did engage the critics, Black, white, male, and female; attract a white audience; and earn a reward for technical expertise—the Pulitzer Prize for Poetry in 1950. Her poetic tale is the embellished bildungsroman (a novel about the moral and psychological growth of the main character) mock-epic of a young, Black, ghetto girl, *Annie Allen,* whose response to the racism and sexism confronting her life is ensconced in complex syntax, classical imagery, and a well-finessed obscurity.

Chapter IV

Annie Allen (1949): The Women of Bronzeville

Brooks' second book of poetry, *Annie Allen* (1949), has received critical attention from three distinctly different theoretical perspectives. Upon its initial publication in 1949, there were mixed reviews from critics whose perceptions were stymied by a book that was so different from her 1945 work, *A Street in Bronzeville.* Namely, Brooks' experimental adaptation of the classic devices of Modernism—form, language, symbol, and myth—created a lingering aura of obscurity that continues to invite astute explications. Secondly, Haki R. Madhubuti (Don L. Lee), one of the most vocal poet-activists of the 1960s' Black Arts Movement, took the book to task because in language, imagery, and technique, Madhubuti, as a representative voice of the Black Power Movement, deemed the book to be directed to a white audience, rather than to Brooks' own cultural constituency, which was a criterion of the Black Aesthetic theory of the 1970s. More recently, in the late 1970s and early 1980s, feminist poet-critics have either ignored or assailed Brooks for her lack of a feminist consciousness. Feminists have perceived Brooks' poetic voice to be distant, rather than personal, and representative of subject, not of self.[1]

Yet the ongoing and burgeoning critical attention devoted to *Annie Allen,* rather than diminish it in importance, has raised it to a level of new critical scrutiny, warranted on one level by the sheer technical expertise and subtle artistic ploys displayed by Brooks. Additionally, in *Annie Allen,* as in *A Street in Bronzeville,* Brooks' meticulous injection of social commentary on the stymied lives of Black women set a literary precedent by breaking the silence that had encumbered the voices of earlier women poets who had long repressed their graphic, intimate, and angry voices.[2] Simultaneous to the challenge for all Black writers to prove their artistic ability by elevating their writing to a universal plane, Brooks, as a Black female poet was doubly challenged by having no visible female role models to blaze a poetic trail. *Annie Allen* is testament to the fact that Brooks met and superseded each challenge; it is for this reason *Annie Allen* must be salvaged and (re)defined as a classic work of art, especially for Black women's literary history.[3]

The first critical audience awaiting the publication of *Annie Allen* (1949) was taken completely by surprise to see the profound differences in this second work and *A Street in Bronzeville* (1945). While Brooks' mastery of prosodic techniques was evident, her experimentation with form, language, and imagery astute, and her narrative intentions apparent, Brooks' quest for a new style was redefined by critics as an excess of classical language, extreme wordplay, and obscure allusions. Many of the reviews had a discordant ring to them, and, at best, yielded mixed assessments from reviewers who found *Annie Allen* inaccessible and whose expectations were so profoundly disturbed by Brooks breaking the artistic mold which produced the Negro character vignettes of *A Street in Bronzeville*, that they vacillated in their assessments, just as her editors at Harper and Row had done in the early stages of production.[4]

An early *Kirkus* reviewer described *Annie Allen* as "refreshing and interesting" [with] "shimmering color and sensuousness . . . warm animal vitality [and] pulsing," but by contrast, wrote: It "doesn't come up to the high standards of the first, it seems less technically competent and precise." Still, he ended on a prophetic note: "There is a quality here long lacking in American poetry. Watch her" (319). Agreeing with that assessment, the *Chicago Sun–Times* critic Leo Kennedy saw Brooks' "brilliant talent" and wrote: "Gwendolyn Brooks is still the latest and finest thing that has happened to Chicago writing since Nelson Algren originally hove in view. . . [*Annie Allen*] is simply lyrical and quite her best work yet" (43). Two other critics who wrote affirming reviews of *Annie Allen* were Phyllis McGinley of the *New York Times Book Review* and Stanley Kunitz in *Poetry*. McGinley wrote: "This is a tender, talented, lyrical little book, uneven, young, and fresh as poetry itself . . . such sophistication of thought and phrase, such vitality" (7). And Kunitz saw "the lively and attractive spirit that sallies forth from her poems" and wrote: "The work of this young Chicago poet never fails to be warmly and generously human" (7). He saw "technical assurance, combined with freshness and spontaneity" and attributed flaws to Brooks' youth: "Like many second books, this is an uneven one. . . . The faults are not faults of incapacity or pretension: what they demonstrate at this stage is an uncertainty of taste and direction" (54).

But there were other critics who were more harsh in their analysis of *Annie Allen*, and especially with Brooks' extensive wordplay. Thomas Hornsby Ferril of the *San Francisco Chronicle* tempered his criticism with a jovial tone:

> [*Annie Allen*] will certainly widen her reputation. This Negro girl does things which can't and mustn't be done: she'll bring in big and impossible poster-words; she loves garish alliteration; but her particular magic makes everything work perfectly. The explanation obvious: She has the keenest sort of mind, and a severe lyrical concreteness is always in control, no matter what extravagant areas of imagination she wanders into. . . . She is really remarkable. (18)

The *New Yorker* wrote briefly: "She has allowed herself in this new volume a good deal of experimentation in language, not all of which comes off" (130).

In the *Saturday Evening Review*, where he played with the same "liquid lyricism" of language he attributes to Brooks,

Saunders Redding saw *Annie Allen* as a "proving" ground for the "valuable poetic gifts" Brooks had evidenced in her first book (23). Initially he assessed the book from an aesthetic vantage point and saw the book as "artistically sure . . . emotionally firm . . .esthetically complete" enhanced by an "intensity. . . richness . . . aptness of imagery [and] glowing warmth" (23). But Redding also saw the book as "racially-particular" and could not accept what he perceived to be an "oblique bitterness" which called into question whether Brooks could afford to be a "coterie poet" (27). And finally, in his most harsh critique, Redding attacked the complexity of *Annie Allen:* "No one wants to read a psychological treatise, or any treatise whatever for that matter, in order to get at the true meaning of a poem. . . . I do not want to see Miss Brooks' fine talents dribble away in the obscure and too oblique" (27). Although Redding saw Brooks' style as "naturally indirect," for him, she is more effective when she "assaults our senses directly" (27).

In a similarly strident, yet balanced assessment, although Babette Deutsch, in the *Yale Review*, saw "relatively fresh subject matter" and "vitality and compassion" in *Annie Allen*, she felt that Brooks "fails to make the most of her material" (363). Specifically, "The Anniad" is "marred by rhetoric" and Brooks "is not so sensitive a craftsman. She tends to use conventional forms with tightly locking rhymes that constrict her unduly, to fit an inappropriate vocabulary to a loose ballad rhythm" (362). Although many of the critical reviews of *Annie Allen* offered thoughtful approaches, keen analysis, and perceptive commentary regarding the obscurity and complexity of Brooks' second work, they did not prevent Brooks from being awarded the Pulitzer Prize for Poetry on May 2, 1950.

Following the rigorous critical examination given *Annie Allen* on the grounds of its modernistic tendencies and linguistic obscurity, the book became the target of cultural critics. The second wave of criticism thrust upon *Annie Allen* is exemplified by the posture of poet-critic Haki Madhubuti (Don L. Lee), a fiery poet of the Black Arts Movement. In the preface to Brooks' first autobiography, *Report From Part One* (1972), Madhubuti dismisses the importance of *Annie Allen* to the Black community and adamantly asserts that the book focuses on "poetic style," rather than "history or tradition" (17), and is targeted to a white audience:

> *Annie Allen* (1949), important? Yes. Read by Blacks? No. *Annie Allen* more so than *A Street in Bronzeville* seems to have been written for whites...Gwendolyn Brooks' ability to use their language while using their ground rules explicitly shows that she far surpassed the best European-Americans had to offer. There is no doubt here. But in doing so, she suffers by not communicating with masses of black people.
> (preface *RPO* 17, 19)

As counterpoint, Madhubuti voices clear appreciation of Brooks' self-redefining post-1967 works, published after her public avowal of a cultural "awakening" and retreat from her former prointegration stance: "Her first and most important contribution was to be the re-directing of her voice to her people—*first and foremost*" (Madhubuti's emphasis, preface *RPO* 22).

The third critical onslaught aimed at Brooks' early poetry which focused on the lives of women, was a school of white, feminist, poet-critics who, in dissonant tones, argue that Brooks has no feminist consciousness. Interestingly enough, it was the early poetic direction Brooks provided, by delving into issues that touched the intimate lives of women, that paved the way for, and informed the current feminist orientation in poetry.

In "The Double Bind of the Woman Poet," feminist critic Suzanne Juhasz opens with the statement that clearly parallels literary history as it dismisses the possibility of early poetic achievement by Black women: "until the twentieth century, there was no body of poetry by women in English" (1). Likewise, in "A Poem of One's Own," Mary Jo Salter bemoans the evidence of "a double-barreled power" propelling men's early poetry, both the "female muse" for inspiration and a male tradition of poetic accomplishment, contrasted to a limited women's poetic tradition: "Women have had a less accomplished literary tradition, though it grows more accomplished every century" (31). She finally acquiesces to touch upon the poetry of Elizabeth Bishop then settles in to rely heavily on Emily Dickinson as her muse and cites research to display Dickinson's affinity for women writers: "Indeed she had read and re-read every Anglo-American woman writer of her time" (32). And Alicia Suskin Ostriker's *Stealing the Language: The Emergence of Women's Poetry in America,* displays a benign neglect of early Black women poets, especially Gwendolyn Brooks, when she discusses the "submerged tradition of women's poetry" (6). Ostriker sets out to examine this "extraordinary tide" of work that "is explicitly female in the sense that the writers have chosen to explore experiences central to their sex and to find forms and styles appropriate to their exploration," with 1960 as her target date (7). By contrast, Juhasz does note Brooks' early critical acclaim: "Gwendolyn Brooks is the only black woman poet to have achieved public and critical recognition before the 1960s" (145).

In an ironic contradiction, Ostriker situates Brooks near the tail-end of a list of poets including Denise Levertov, Adrienne Rich, Anne Sexton, and Sylvia Plath, whose first books were published after Brooks' 1945 and 1949 works. She then cites Brooks' 1960 and 1963 works, the latter of which, *Selected Poems*, encompasses the larger portion of her earlier publications. Indeed, of the eighty-five poems in *Selected Poems*, fifty-one were published prior to 1960. In a nebulous reference, Ostriker includes Brooks in the early white women and Black women who, in the twentieth century contributed, "a steady stream of political poetry" before 1945 (55).[5] Still later, Ostriker notes that "the mother as an autonomous figure has been excluded from literature," then, finally acknowledges Brooks' 1945 attention to women's topics: "Gwendolyn Brooks' widely anthologized poem 'The Mother' is actually an abortion poem whose speaker articulates complex feelings of yearning, loss, guilt, and love toward the children she got but did not get" (180).

The feminist perspectives of Juhasz, Salter, and Ostriker strike the eerie bell chord of exclusion that has persistently swung past Brooks' poetic contributions, especially odd since much of Brooks' early work focuses on women's issues of menial labor, abortion, and sexism. Rather, Juhasz pays specific attention to what she perceives to be a lack of a feminist "self" in Brooks' poetry. Juhasz concentrates on the "peculiar tension" that resulted in the "madness" and suicides of Sylvia Plath and Anne Sexton as indicative of white women poets who are ill-equipped to withstand the onslaught of conflicts poured on them for the "double-bind" of "being both woman and artist" in a world of creativity that respects and even demands "masculine characteristics"(3). She writes: "The conflict between her two 'selves' is an excruciating and irreconcilable civil war, when both sides are in fact the same person" (2). To set her feminist stage, Juhasz appropriates W. E. B. Du Bois' social theory of the "double-consciousness" of Black Americans in order to authenticate the feminist bind of white women poets by situating it in close proximity to the recognized tradition of stark alienation and rampant discrimination inflicted upon Black Americans. She co-ops the thinking of critic Louis Simpson from a 1963 *New York Herald Tribune* review of Brooks' *Selected Poems* where he asserted: "if being Negro is the only subject, the writing is not important" (27), when she states, "If the poet 'writes like a man,' she denies her own experience; if she writes as a woman, her subject matter is trivial" (3).

In an attempt to deconstruct any manifestation of feminism in Brooks' work, Juhasz attempts to align Black women poets along the same continuum of white women's oppression by assigning a "triple-bind" of "race and sex oppression" as the barrier that stymies Black women writers: "she [the Black woman poet] experiences conflicts between being poet and woman, poet and black, black and woman" (145). Thus, for Juhasz, race not only supersedes gender in importance for the Black woman poet, it completely demolishes any inclination for a feminist perspective. She writes: "[Brooks'] blackness has stayed three steps ahead of womanhood" (4). Similarly, Kate Daniels sees a "feminist conflict" that is more pronounced for Black women writers. In "The Demise of the 'Delicate Prisons': The Women's Movement in Twentieth-Century American Poetry," she writes:

> If every female writer finds herself, as I have suggested, in a double bind of perplexity about the nature of female genius in a profoundly male-dominated society, how much more complicated is that bind for women writers of color who find themselves at every turn confronted by the deforming pressures of racism? (244)

Yet Audre Lorde is a prime example of Black women who refused to be pigeon-holed on the question of feminine identity. In an interview with Claudia Tate, she asserts her identity with unmistakable clarity: "I am a Black, Lesbian, Feminist, Warrior, Mother, lover, woman, poet doing my work" (100). Likewise, the question of problematic prioritizing of personal versus artistic identity that Juhasz and Daniels define for white women writers is not replicated in the lives of other Black women writers, especially not Brooks. In "Gwendolyn the Terrible: Propositions on Eleven Poems," Hortense Spillers defines Brooks by her poetic presence:

> We cannot always say with grace or ease that there is a direct correspondence between the issues of her poetry and her race and sex, nor does she make the assertion necessary at every step of our reading. Black and female are basic and inherent in her poetry. (224)

And, in a self-defining act, Brooks states simply: "I am an ordinary human being who is impelled to write poetry" (*RPO* 135).

Though Juhasz acknowledges Brooks' race consciousness and poetic craft, she expresses concern that Brooks has not availed herself of a decidedly feminist orientation: "Over the years, Brooks has developed a black consciousness; in her fifties, she opened herself to revolution. But she has not developed at the same time a feminist consciousness" (150). Juhasz is concerned that despite the distinct feminine consciousness that is apparent throughout Brooks' entire canon, Brooks has not adapted her poetic craft to a feminist discourse that reveres the personal voice of the poet, the evidence of the "I" or "self," or the intimate rendering of the female body in a personalized discourse.[6] Brooks' attention to the prison of domestic employment that holds "Hattie Scott" captive, the sexist treatment battled by the "Queen of the Blues," and the rebellion against social norms in "Sadie and Maud," (*A Street in Bronzeville*) simply do not measure up to the strictures and structures established by the white feminist poet-critics. As Juhasz writes: "[Brooks] has a vested interest in women attaining strength and independence, but her interest in them as a group is not political. Women have always been prominent as subject matter for her poems, but she has written about them as about everything else, as subject, never as self" (151). Juhasz frets over the "distance" in Brooks' voice in "The Anniad": "Brooks at no time speaks in a personal or a private voice. She is a dramatic poet, speaking either in the voice of a character . . . or in the voice of an author who does not participate in the drama directly. . . .

She does not speak in the lyric voice . . . the voice of the self" (151). At this point in her analysis, Juhasz begins to vacillate because she is confused about where to place Brooks:

> Like the white women of her generation, Brooks may write about women, but rarely will she include herself among them. She never achieves either the personalism or the engagement that I have identified with the 'feminine' poet. Yet there is a difference between her presentation of women and that of the white women poets who are her contemporaries: in Brooks' poetry—and indeed, throughout the poetry of black women—there is a pride in womanhood that does not exist in the poetry of white women until recently. (154)

Where white women poets have needed to see themselves as somehow "special," removed from the mundane tasks of domesticity and motherhood, "essentially weak creatures whose life-style she repudiated for the sake of her art," Black women have always exuded strength, as wives, as mothers, and as artists (154).[7] What Juhasz misses, in an act of racial hegemony, is that white feminist inclinations do not necessarily set the tone or example for Black women. The fact that Brooks' manner of confronting issues of critical importance to an audience of women does not mimic the personal voice of the self subscribed to by many white feminist critics, is no reason to assume that that voice is not "heard" as the voice of the self by Black women who must establish their own parameters of feminism, regardless of the directions established by white feminists whose lived experiences might be vastly different.[8]

Similarly, Salter takes up the issue of domesticity and its dire effects on women writers, noting that traditionally fiction-writing has been easier for the childless woman writer:

> Most women writers of fiction in history have been childless, and it is only now that we can amass a long list of distin-

> guished women fiction writers and remark with nothing less than joy at how many are mothers...The list of the best women poets in our language, by contrast, is a nearly unbroken catalog of childlessness. (34)

She goes on to catalog a list of white writers including Emily Dickinson, Marianne Moore, and Elizabeth Bishop and concludes: "If we take comfort in remembering that Sylvia Plath was a mother, it is not for long: we know what happened to her" (34). Salter is very disturbed at "the dearth of excellent mother-poets" since the implication is that women writers have traded in their ability to be mothers for that of being writers (34).[9]

No Black women writers are mentioned in the article although Gwendolyn Brooks, Audre Lorde, Toni Morrison, and Alice Walker all have children and have been consistent writers. This quiet, but persistent sweeping aside of Black women when the issues of women writers are discussed is not only discomforting when it comes from avowed feminists, but points to the different orientation of Black and white women writers. Adrienne Rich appears to be somewhat more grounded in her feminist-poet identity than her white feminist poet-critic sisters. She too voices concern at the dual tasks of motherhood and artistic realization in her essay "When We Dead Awaken: Writing as Re-Vision."[10] After marriage and three children in rapid succession, she writes of her fledgling poetic inclinations:

> I was writing very little, partly from fatigue, that female fatigue of suppressed anger and loss of contact with my own being; partly from the discontinuity of female life with its attention to small chores, errands, work that others constantly undo, small children's constant needs . . . I want to make it clear that I am *not* saying that in order to write well, or think well, it is necessary to become unavailable to others, or to become a devouring ego. This has been the myth of the masculine artist and thinker; and I do not accept it. But to be a female human being trying to fulfill traditional female

> functions in a traditional way *is* in direct conflict with the subversive function of the imagination. (Rich's emphasis 43)

In a final expression of her frustration, Rich writes: "I wanted, then, more than anything, the one thing of which there was never enough: time to think, time to write" (44).

But on the subject of a "divided-self," the dual tensions of domesticity and artistry, and the need to choose, Brooks responded to a question posed in a *Great Lakes Review* interview conducted by Martha H. Brown that unlike the conflicts of being a wife and mother that assailed poet-mother Sylvia Plath, she was very much at ease with juggling dual roles: "I feel that writing is part of life. I often say that poetry is 'life distilled,' and I believe that's true of any other aspect of writing. Being a wife and mother and having other interests in life did not do anything except enrich my work—nourish it" (48). And on the subject of her own time management, novelist Toni Morrison broadens the discussion in a Claudia Tate interview: "Time has never really been a problem for me . . . I can do two things at once" (119). She then proceeds to delineate the differences in Black and white women's writing:

> It seems to me there's an enormous difference in the writing of black and white women. Aggression is not as new to black women as it is to white women. Black women seem able to combine the nest and the adventure. They don't see conflicts in certain areas as do white women. They are both safe harbor and ship; they are both inn and trail. We, black women, do both. We don't find these places, these roles, mutually exclusive. That's one of the differences. White women often find if they leave their husbands and go out into the world, it's an extraordinary event. If they've settled for the benefits of housewifery that preclude a career, then it's marriage *or* a career for them, not both, not *and*. (Tate's emphasis 122)

Morrison's perspective on the different ways in which Black and white women write adds clarity to the independence Brooks has persistently displayed in the theme and execution of her poetry. There is no indication that she has ever been encumbered as a Black-woman-mother-poet. By contrast, Brooks' works, from 1945 to 1960, represent her ever increasing awareness of America's social climate and her need to comment on the oppressive forces impacting her community, especially its women.

Having perused the disparate ways in which Black and white women write, the response of Brooks' poetic peers Robert Hayden and Melvin Tolson to the literary mandates of the day, and the social and literary conditions contributing to the climate in which Brooks wrote *Annie Allen*, there is still a lingering question. Why did Brooks opt to approach the story of women—motherhood, daughterhood, and womanhood—from such a complex technical perspective? In "Race, Black Women Writing, and Gwendolyn Brooks," Betsy Erkkila offers an astute analysis of the source of Brooks' poetic tradition:

> What is striking about Brooks' years of literary apprenticeship is her relative lack of anxiety about setting up as a black female singer in comparison with the turmoil and self-division that has characterized white women poets from Anne Bradstreet to Adrienne Rich. This relative lack of conflict is all the more striking because Brooks had no visible black female poetic precursors. . . . Brooks' emergence as a poet must be understood within the context of her personal and cultural experience as an African American woman. (193)[11]

The fact that Brooks had no visible Black female literary tradition to draw upon as a model for emulation or inspiration is evident in recent works that strive to uncover the women poets who wrote and published between the time of Phillis Wheatley and the Harlem Renaissance.[12] Instead, Brooks initially developed her poetic craft by her exposure to the "Big Three" of the Harlem Renaissance, McKay, Cullen, and Hughes; Inez Stark, a white North Side socialite and former reader for *Poetry* magazine; and James Weldon Johnson, who, along with Stark, encouraged Brooks' study of the Modernist poets.[13] But the poet who was pivotal in Brooks' life, Langston Hughes, steered her in the direction of a familiar milieu when he urged Brooks to look at the "ordinary aspects of black life" for inspiration, which, says Brooks, is what Hughes did (*RPO* 170):

> Mightily did he use the street. He found its multiple heart, its tastes, smells, alarms, formulas, flowers, garbage and convulsions. He brought them all to his table-top. He crushed them to a writing-paste. He himself became the pen. (71)

And Brooks had done just that in her first book of poetry. From her various "kitchenette" apartments, she had recorded the sights and sounds of Bronzeville in poems like "The Sundays of Satin-Legs Smith" and "of De Witt Williams on his way to Lincoln Cemetery." As she states, "If you wanted a poem, you had only to look out of a window. There was material always, walking or running, fighting or screaming or singing" (*RPO* 69).

But for *Annie Allen*, Brooks needed to look for a different source of inspiration from ordinary life, so she turned to a more personal subject: the stymied lives of Black ghetto women. The vast reservoir of material from the Black male writers of the Harlem Renaissance was of little value to Brooks in terms of looking at a female literary tradition, and though there was a circle of women writing and publishing regularly in journals, only Georgia Douglas Johnson had published in book form.[14] The patronage system that supported the flowering of the Harlem Renaissance was "a white-sponsored and black male-centered production" (Erkkila 187). But Brooks was not without resources.

She could invert the spirit of her own childhood as a social commentary on the lives of women suffering from racist and sexist oppression. Brooks could rely on the lingering memories of her most cherished and familiar source of support and love—the rich lives of the women who surrounded her as a young girl. She had a ripe storehouse of family traditions and memories—the pungent Christmas fruitcakes, the singing of carols, and the "scrupulous housecleaning"—that spelled togetherness and love (41); she had the warmth and love exuded by her mother whom she remembers for her "love of gardening" (47): Home meant everything to young Brooks:

> Home, however, warmly awaited me. Welcoming, enveloping. Home meant a quick-walking, careful, Duty-Loving mother, who played the piano, made fudge, made cocoa and prune whip and apricot pie, drew tidy cows and trees and expert houses with chimneys and chimney smoke, who helped her children with arithmetic homework, and who sang in a high soprano: "Brighten the corner where you are!. . . How happy was I!" (39, 41)

A bonus to the catalogue of family sharing for special events, like the Easter egg hunts, Halloween, and birthdays, were the cherished interactions with her aunts. Among these maternal and paternal aunts, one had a warm personality and a home that expressed "merriment," because of her "repasts impressive to one's taste-buds"; another "helpful" aunt filled "empty jelly jars" with "pennies, nickels, dimes and quarters . . . for a savings bond"; a third "was childless," and helped "other people's children"; and finally two aunts were "proficient" in sewing, and one "made so many dresses for me that my parents didn't need to purchase any during the first seven years of my life" (48).

The glow Brooks exudes about the women in her family, especially her mother, challenges those women writers who express concern that the subject of mother-daughter relationships has not yet found a home in women's writing. In 1945, Brooks saw the oppressive conditions that negatively impacted the lives of all Black people, with an especially stultifying effect on the lives of Black women. A recent work, by Patricia Bell-Scott and others, *Double Stitch: Black Women Write About Mothers and Daughters*, was published because there was a need to explore the complexity of these relationships. Bell-Scott writes: "relationships between Black mothers and daughters are profoundly affected by the subtleties as well as the brutalities of sexism within and without African-American communities" (xiv).[15] Brooks' weapon of confrontation against the oppressive conditions regulating women's lives is language, the power of the poetic word as social commentary. In "Afro-American Women Poets," Barbara Christian writes:

> Brooks has always written about women—how they see themselves, as mothers and daughters, wives and lovers, as restricted or fulfilled. And her work has always focused on the sexist expressions of racism in this country. Yet Brooks would not consider herself a woman poet. She does not protest the restrictive conditions of women's lives so much as she presents the complexity of their existence. (123)

Actually, Brooks does both. Under the guise of the technical proficiency and craftsmanship that was the mandate for prointegrationist Black writers of the 1940s, Brooks creates a poetics so obscure that even for the women whose lives are stricken by racism and sexism, the message must be deciphered. Brooks constructs a mask—a delicate veil of subterfuge—to subvert her message of social commentary.

In *Black Sister: Poetry By Black American Women*, Erlene Stetson argues compellingly that Black women poets use three "creative strategies" to confront the injustice and oppression in their lives:

> As a logical result of the social forces in their lives, carried on under the practical travesty of "liberty and justice for all," black women poets in the United States have been driven into a compelling quest for identity because they are denied "cultural wholeness." (xviii)

The weapons of survival identified by Stetson are visible in the poetry of Brooks: "a compelling quest for identity" in a world that renders Black women poets invisible, "a subversive perception of reality" that the perception of the American creed for Black Americans is not a reality, and finally, "subterfuge and ambivalence" as a response to the denial of forthright self-expressions of protest (xviii).

In *Annie Allen*, Brooks dares to mock poetic conventions and address the ill-treatment of a young naive ghetto girl by infusing her consciousness with the lofty diction and romantic imagery of classical poetry. *Annie Allen* is a protest of the meager status of Black women in American society, yet there are specific poems that speak most directly to their skewed lives. The formal arrangement of three segments represents Annie's life from birth, to youth, and finally to womanhood. Each segment contributes to the full expression of the bildungsroman, or coming-of-age, motif, like the mother-daughter tug-of-war for control of Annie's life in the first segment, "Notes From the Childhood and the Girlhood," and Annie's decision to meet life on its own terms in the final segment, "The Womanhood." But it is in the central poem of the work, "The Anniad," that Brooks most cogently subverts the "newness" of the Modernist poetics to sing of a woman's pain—but survival, a feat that must be recorded in poetic history as a road map for other victims of racial and sexual oppression who are struggling to escape the maze of injustices. Gertrude Reif Hughes defines that "newness" in "Making it *Really* New: Hilda Doolittle, Gwendolyn Brooks, and the Feminist Potential of Modern Poetry," when she identifies the imagism, synchronicity, antiheroic sensibility, and obscurity as the "four poetic elements of masculinist modernism" Brooks subverts to "protest oppressive practices" and expose "the misogyny of romance conventions" (376).

With the opening poem from "Notes From the Childhood and the Girlhood," "the birth in a narrow room," Brooks abruptly begins playing with the Modernist tools of compression and economy of language in the opening lines of the sestet: "Weeps out of western country something new. / Blurred and stupendous. Wanted and unplanned" (83). Foreshadowing and word-play are the dominant devices that control the movement and meaning of the poem. A concealed narrator announces the cry of childbirth as Annie "weeps" her way into a life that foreshadows strife and repression, symbolized by the tension of the "narrow room" and juxtaposed against the "stupendous" and "unplanned" birth that simultaneously hint at the romantic outlook that will ultimately manipulate her perception of life. In the lines that follow, it is clear that for Annie, life is only momentarily idyllic: "The bashful china child tipping forever / Yellow apron and spilling pretty cherries" (83).

Brooks' use of imagery supports the coming oppression of Annie's adult life as the romantic vision of the "milk-glass fruit bowl" dissipates into a solid bump with the reality of "old peach cans and old jelly jars" in the final line. The early happiness of her life is swept aside rapidly as Annie feels the encroaching compression of her life:

> Now, weeks and years will go before she thinks
> "How pinchy is my room! how can I breathe!
> I am not anything and I have got
> Not anything, or anything to do!"— (83)

In the early lines of the poem, the alliteration of the infant Annie's "Winks. Twines, and weakly winks" signals hope for a new evolving life and expanding vision, while "pinchy" is a metaphor for the stymied adult life awaiting Annie with the twin fangs of racism and sexism.

The hope that Annie can gain sufficient survival tools to overcome the ravages of ghetto life rests squarely on the shoulders of her mother, Maxie Allen. In the poem "Maxie Allen," Annie and her mother are caught in the cross fire of hope and defeat, with the mother being agitated at the failures of her own life, pitted against the incessant barrage of Annie's youthful, unfulfilled fancies. The first of three ten-line stanzas begins a communication between the mother and daughter that establishes a subtle "call and response" sermonic pattern.[16] In the first stanza, the narrator expresses the feelings of the didactic mother toward "her / Stipendiary little Daughter" who should "thank her Lord and lucky star" for life's basics, including "Her Quaker Oats and Cream-of-Wheat . . . [and] penny" (84). In stanza two, "Sweet Annie's" idyllic response to life is stifled by her realization that life holds more than she is getting, although: "She did not know; but tried to tell." The final stanza reveals the climax of the heated debate: In a "bedeviling" voice like "an oceanic thing," the mother finally admits in her own first-person voice that unlike Annie, who at least has "lots of jacks and strawberry jam," her own life is pitifully dismal (84).

Form supports meaning as Brooks establishes the romanticism of the tetrameter line for the rhythm of Annie's imaginative hopefulness, held in check by the nagging "something other." The rhymed couplets suggest the same call-and-response pattern in the ongoing sparring between mother and daughter. The insistent end rhymes reach for the optimism that is implied by Annie's willingness to settle for "just a deep and human look."

But the "settling" implied in the poem "the parents: people like our marriage / Maxie and Andrew" is an ironic manipulation of memory that foreshadows Annie's grandiose dreams of a chivalric knight. The opening of the poem wanders into the gentle memory of more spirited times: "Clogged and soft and sloppy eyes / Have lost the light that bites or terrifies" (86). "Swans and swallows" are the elegant dreams on which the parents have "shut the door" and "settled for chicken" (86). In sharp contrast to Annie's romantic notions, the parents have "settled" for a bland and boring, but acceptable life: "Pleasant custards sit behind / The white Venetian blind" (86). Ironically, the mundane existence of Annie's parents is juxtaposed against the "something other" Annie craves in "Maxie Allen" and realized in the dual themes of compliance and betrayal between Annie and her chivalric knight of "The Anniad."

Foreshadowing continues to be the harbinger of the impending conflicts of Annie's life in the poems "the ballad of late Annie," "do not be afraid of no," and "my own sweet good." The opening ballad stanza of "the ballad of late Annie" is a portrait of Annie's mythologizing about a man of "gist and lacquer" who will be "chief enough" to marry her, foreshadowing the arrival of the "paladin" in "The Anniad":

> Late Annie in her bower lay,
> Though sun was up and spinning.
> The blush-brown shoulder was so bare,
> Blush-brown lip was winning. (90)

The "late" of the title signals Annie's reluctance, even resistance, to release the reins of childhood and face the portentous reality "shrieked" at her by the forceful "mother-dear": "Get a broom to whish the doors / Or get a man to marry." Unlike the "call and response" sparring of Annie and her mother in "Maxie Allen," here Annie resists the admonitions of her mother by remaining inert; thus, she avoids the confrontation implied in "do not be afraid of no." As indicative of the "languid, dormant, and unresisting character" Claudia Tate argues for in "Anger So Flat: Gwendolyn Brooks' *Annie Allen*," Annie's act of sleeping encodes a ritual of passivity that transfers her psychological and emotional energies to the fecund imagination that creates and awaits her "paladin."[17]

Brooks' use of form and language in "the ballad of late Annie" is strategic to the success of the mock-heroics that will reemerge in and control "The Anniad." First, her use of the ballad form endows Annie with the heroic stature that supports Annie's contemplation of a man of equal stature. Second, Annie lies, not in her bed, but in her medieval "bower," as the whimsical assertion of the force of her imaginary life. Brooks then imposes newness by counterpoising the stilted archaic language of the English ballad against the dual usages, formal and colloquial, of "fetch," and "cracker." The harsh voiced mother questions Annie: "Be I to fetch and carry?" And the final two lines of the poem confirm Brooks' dual purpose as she plays the language against itself when the man of "gist and lacquer" approaches Annie: "With melted opals for my milk, / Pearl-leaf for my cracker" (90).

A second forecast of Annie's impending doom is driven home in syntactically diverted language that suggests the utter chaos of women's lives in "'do not be afraid of no.'" The poem opens with a perplexing quotation: "'Do not be afraid of no, / Who has so far so very far to go'": (92). Though the question of speaker and addressee surfaces immediately, it is finally the devastating effects of saying "yes" that insistently drive home the cautionary message that saying "no" can be equated with human survival, in contrast to "the ballad of late Annie" which suggests that because the mock-heroine is ill-prepared to tackle life on its own terms, she has said "yes" to a life of romantic illusions.

Structurally the poem recalls Brooks' formal instruction with Inez Stark who, in view of Brooks' early attempts at poetry, had urged: "Dig at this until you have us see all the skeleton and no fat" (*RPO* 67).[18] Brooks complies with the Modernist convention of thrusting newness on old forms by nestling any easy interpretation of the recent "just say no" vogue in a series of grammatical fragments that demands close analysis, and according to Barksdale, simply leads to "grammatical confusion" ("Poetry" 413).[19] The word of "caution" in the second stanza is directed to a vague "her" who just might find it easier to yield to life's easy material gains than moral dictates: "New caution to occur / To one whose inner scream set her to cede, for softer lapping / and smooth fur!" (92).

Meaning gains momentum as the speaker graphically depicts the kind of "nettle" the addressee can "avoid" by learning to say "no." To say "yes" would define a "stupid" individual who would use a mere "candle" to navigate sheer bedlam:

> Wild moon and sun. And like
> A flying furniture, or bird with lattice wing; or gaunt thing,
> a-stammer down a nightmare neon peopled with condor, hawk and shrike. (92)

Saying "yes" "is to die / A lot or a little," to be remembered only by a decorated headstone, a "smell," and silence. Brooks drives the message home by a vigorous use of alliteration in "Stupid, like a street," the symbolism of the "candle," and the final internal and terminal rhyme of "smell . . . yell . . . well" as dismissal to one who would be so trite as to enter the "dead end" street of con(cede)ing to saying "yes."

On the other hand, saying "no" offers the distinct moral fiber of character and integrity to one who would be so "brave" and noble. Though the poetic discussion of saying "yes" has commanded eight of ten stanzas, it is the final two that bear testament to the intended directive. Formally, line sequence attains a regularity in obvious contrast to the linear irregularity of the earlier rhymed couplets so that clarity and brevity finally signal meaning: "It is brave to be involved, / To be not fearful to be unresolved." Annie has now been set on the proper course to face the trials that await her in "The Anniad," and overcome them in "The Womanhood."[20]

The final forecast of the imminent arrival of Annie's "paladin" is the poem "my own sweet good" where the concealed narrator projects Annie's sense of clarity about the frivolous nature and needs of the man:

> "Not needing, really, my own sweet good,
> To dimple you every day,
> For knowing you roam like a gold half-god
> And your golden promise was gay." (95)

Polyptoton and bluesy repetition relentlessly drive home the dazzling attraction of the "gold half-god" with the ending line of each stanza being a variation on the theme: "golden and gay." First, Annie's awareness and acceptance that the unnamed man, who will remain unnamed in "the Anniad," resides in a vague "somewhere," co-mingle with the knowledge that he strays in her direction sporadically: "Ill-knowing your route rides to me, roundabout." Additionally, her cognizance of his other romantic ventures: "You kiss all the great-lipped girls that you can," will be further explored in "The Anniad" as the "paladin" wanders from one sexual or romantic alliance to another.

"The Anniad"

The apex of *Annie Allen* is the mock-epic "The Anniad." Brooks makes a mockery of prosodic and linguistic traditions by exploiting poetic form and language to depict the pretentiousness of social conditions for Black Americans, and especially for women. Although the stanzaic pattern of "The Anniad" may be likened to the classical rhyme royal and the "quick rhythms" to ottava rima, these structural similarities merely suggest Brooks' easy familiarity with traditional forms; in reality, Brooks' intentional divergences, such as the missing invocation, the modified stanzaic versions, the substitution of tetrameter, and her alteration to rhyme and half-rhyme, suggest her explicit defiance of any semblance of adherence to poetic form and thus signal her intentional deviance from the strictures of classical prosody (62–3).[21] Additionally the shifting tone of the work, from compassion, mockery, irony, sarcasm, ridicule, disdain and finally, to compassion again, suggests the use of satire as a strategy for embedding the strident voice of social criticism in a work of art that is "uncompromisingly beautiful, yet socially responsible."[22]

Annie Allen is the tale of an urban Black girl who is struggling with her own emerging womanhood in the midst of a society which has taught her to look with disfavor upon her skin color and hair texture and to seek ideals for both her standard of beauty and prospective husband from classic European representations. Because the poet-narrator and Annie have been educated by a system comprised solely of Euro-American models, the lofty diction, allusive imagery, and prosodic techniques bear a greater resemblance to European culture, than to the colloquial vernacular and stark imagery of Annie's ghetto environment.[23]

The irony is that while a surface inspection of the poem might yield the consensus that "The Anniad" is a "white" poem, Brooks subverts her message of social commentary in structural variations and prosodic complexities to criticize the social system which created the inequality Annie and her male suitor endure as a fact of Black life in America. In "The Achievement of Gwendolyn Brooks," Houston Baker likens Brooks' writing to that of W. E. B. Du Bois: "The high style of both authors...is often used to explicate the condition of the black American trapped behind a veil that separates him from the white world" (23). With "The Anniad," Brooks successfully targeted and attracted a white audience who would recognize, appreciate, and reward her poetic efforts, while she simultaneously vented her social concerns under the veil of "double-consciousness."

The poet-narrator of "The Anniad" explores the emotionally charged themes of war, disease, infidelity, and death as they immediately impact the life of a Black ghetto man, and subsequently reverberate on the imagination, life, and memory of a Black ghetto woman, Annie Allen, as a measure of the sexist treatment of women in society and a protest against that treatment. In the first of forty-three stanzas, Annie Allen is introduced with particular emphasis on her lowly stature and impoverished condition made more palatable to her by a rich imagination:

> Think of sweet and chocolate,
> Left to folly or to fate,
> Whom the higher gods forgot,
> Whom the lower gods berate;
> Physical and underfed
> Fancying on the featherbed
> What was never and is not. (99)

The first five stanzas of "The Anniad" concentrate on the lowly position Annie occupies both in society and in her own life and offers a social commentary on the criteria of both dominant white society and the Black community for establishing the worth of human beings.

For the first of seven times in the poem, with the voice of the poet-narrator as guide, the reader is admonished to "Think of" Annie, in a directive that establishes the nature of protest in the poem.[24] These stanzas initially inspire a mythological vision of a young Black girl who is "sweet," but whose "fate" has already been decided by "the higher gods" of the dominate white society, as well as "the lower gods" of her own Black cultural community. Though Annie's "buxom berries" and "ripe and rompabout . . . harvest" (99) announce her ascendancy to the threshold of womanhood, her "unembroidered brown" and "black and boisterous hair" (100) suggest a devaluing of her physical attributes by a society that rejects "chocolate" skin and natural hair as appealing standards of beauty. Brooks confirms that stance in "XIII, Intermission, 3" when the poet narrator addresses Annie: "Stand off, daughter of the dusk, / And do not wince when the bronzy lads / Hurry to cream-yellow shining" (137) and in earlier poems, like "the ballad of chocolate Mabbie," "patent leather," "at the hairdresser's," and "Ballad of Pearl May Lee," where skin color and hair texture are paramount to societal acceptance.[25] Because Annie is "emotionally aware" of her precarious plight, she is "taming all that anger down," by diverting her whimsical musings to an imaginary romantic knight, the "paladin," who, she believes, will arrive to quench her imaginative thirst and "rub her secrets out" (99). But "The Anniad's" final line of stanza one, "What is never and is not" (99), converges with the first line of stanza two, "What is ever and is not" (99), to foreshadow the "fate" of Annie's adult life with emphatic terminal repetition.

In stanzas six through eight, "The Anniad's" poet-narrator introduces the sophisticated, worldly, and versatile "man of tan" who in Annie's naivete is the "Prosperous and ocean-eyed," "Ruralist and rather bad," "Cosmopolitan and kind" paladin of her romantic dreams (100). Metaphorical imagery virtually blossoms in the poem, becoming increasingly significant as both Annie and the "man of tan" are equated with various elements of nature. Annie's virginal quality is equated with the newness and freshness of "green" and the "springtime of her pride" (100), while the "man of tan" is likened to an animal who "Eats" away at Annie's innocence with "intimidating teeth" (100). Later, the "green" of Annie's youth and sexual innocence is redefined as the disease and sexual carousing that spell death for her lover (103).

In stanza eight, the poet-narrator makes it clear that Annie is "consume[d]" by this man of limited scope as she blindly bestows god-like qualities upon her "Narrow master master," though even he is bewildered by his undeserved stature (100).

> How he postures at his height;
> Unfamiliar, to be sure,
> With celestial furniture.
> Contemplating by cloud-light
> His bejeweled diadem;
> As for jewels, counting them,
> Trying if the pomp be pure. (100)

The artificiality of Annie's idealistic vision is defined both by the oxymoron of her "gilt humility" for her preening lover and the images of his stunning surface qualities which will reappear as the "fictive gold that mocks" him in his life of sexual carousing (100, 108).

The lover's casual denigration of Annie establishes his sexist perception of women as convenient objects for his personal use and foreshadows his penchant for the random selection of women. With an eye to frugality, he defiles her in a "lowly room" that "his pocket chooses," while Annie conducts a "metamorphosis" of it as "a chapel" where she "genuflects to love" (101). The lover's easy mockery of Annie's sexuality later inflates to gigantic proportions as his sexual dalliances make him view her in an increasingly harsh light; when he returns from war and seeks a woman to compensate for his feelings of inadequacy, his sneer is a haughty dismissal of Annie: "Not that woman! (Not that room! / Not that dusted demi-gloom!) / Nothing limpid, nothing meek" (104).

"The Anniad" reaches a crescendo of semantic compression and complexity as war intrudes upon the landscape of romanticism. The sporadic omission of nouns, pronouns, verbs, articles, and deictics is especially pronounced in stanzas twelve through fourteen as a commentary on the violent and chaotic climate of war. Spillers offers the enticing view that "the quality of images in 'The Anniad'. . . is auditory rather than visual, because Brooks, as well as the reader, is so thoroughly fascinated with the sound of words" (230). The mythological creations of Annie's mind, juxtaposed at every turn by the realities of the unnamed and unworthy man, become mired in complex apocalyptic imagery as the antihero is drafted to war. Language that has been stilted and often archaic in previous stanzas, now jars the senses with virtual incomprehensibility as the poet-narrator decries the horrors of war:[26]

> Doomer, though, crescendo-comes
> Prophesying hecatombs.
> Surrealist and cynical.
> Garrulous and guttural.
> Spits upon the silver leaves.
> Denigrates the dainty eves
> Dear dexterity achieves. (101)

But Brooks counterpoises the pointlessness of war against the explicit act of defining that occurs for Black men. For the unnamed "man of tan," war "Names him. Tames him. Takes him off"; it empowers him with an identity. He is a soldier who must now answer the "reveille" war cry of a "staccato majesty" and adhere to the rigors of military discipline that will prepare him for "The hunched hells across the sea" (102). The empowering "drama" of war, created and controlled by white male power, is shortlived for tan man; when he returns home, no longer permitted to "act out" his part, and thrust into his old ill-fitting garb of second-class citizenship, the tone of social criticism seizes the poem: "Hometown hums with stoppages...And this white and greater chess / Baffles tan man" (103). Ironically, war has exercised much of the same callous disregard for tan man that he exercised over "sweet" Annie; his body has been exposed to and ravished by disease, leaving him with a portentous "green / Moist sweet breath" that hints at tuberculosis, and his spirit is broken:

> With his helmet's final doff
> Soldier lifts his power off.
> Soldier bare and chilly then
> Wants his power back again. (103)

The stanza locates tan man's military prowess, as well as his sexual explorations abroad. He has not only been stripped of the military paternity that gave him some semblance of power and identity, but also a male identity greatly enhanced by the sweet, lazy, and sensual indulgences implied by the final lines of the stanza: "No confection languider / Before quick-feast quick-famish Men / Than the candy crowns-that-were" (103). He now needs something to replace the vigor he felt in war and "Hunts a further fervor now" to alleviate his "impotence" (103).

Though he runs to Annie for solace and "Tosses to her lap entire" (102) after the devastating effects of war, he ultimately rejects the "meek" Annie for more exotic "bad honey" women who are reminiscent of his overseas encounters (104); and Annie must seek solace in other realms (105–106). During his carousing, tan man gets a "gorgeous and gold shriek" of a woman who hisses erotically and coils like a snake; he "Gets a maple banshee. Gets / A sleek slit-eyed gypsy moan" and parties wildly with a "mad bacchanalian lass" in the drunken revelry of his "random passion" as he desperately attempts to salvage some semblance of the military or sexual power that has been stripped from him (104). Ultimately, however, all that tan man gets is death. He eventually "Stiffens: yellows" (103) from his "overseas disease," the "scenic bacchanal" of his drunken orgies, the "Wench, whiskey and tail-end / Of [his] overseas disease" that take their toll on his debilitated body (107).

But while the tan man is in the midst of his drunken revelry, the poet-narrator abruptly returns to inspect the emotional isolation of Annie's mundane life; anaphora confirms the dearth of fun and activity that is an explicit contrast to tan man's life:

> Think of sweet and chocolate
> Minus passing-magistrate,
> Minus passing-lofty light,
> Minus passing-stars for night,
> Sirocco wafts and tra la la,
> Minus symbol, cinema
> Mirages, all things suave and bright. (104)

In stanzas twenty-four through thirty-one, a more curious Annie emerges who begins to test the waters of life, augmented by a parallel formal change to a persistent trochaic meter and an active verb sequence at each stanza opening. An otherwise passive and inert Annie now "Seeks" "Runs" "Spins" "Sends" "Twists" "Tests" in a move of self-consolation and enlightenment that may be interpreted as her first step toward emotional survival, even as she seeks a balm for the pain caused by her self-serving lover.

The nature imagery of seasonal changes dominates the central section of the poem as Annie gropes for comfort in the rich winter imagery of the real "jewels" of nature that "glint and glow" in "blue and silver," versus the "fictive gold" of her relationship with tan man (105). In the "green and fluting spring," she seeks regeneration, but is halted in her reverie by the foreshadowing of death when the ominous "Hyacinthine devils sing" and the fresh atmosphere of spring is spoiled by evil spirits: "unseen / Pucks and cupids make a fine / Fume of fondness and sunshine" (105). The pace of her search for solace heats up as she "Runs to summer" only to be mocked in her aloneness by the enveloping sensuality of the "Heavy and inert . . . heat" that "hoots at solitaire" (105). By fall, Annie is loosing her grip on reality as she "Runs to parks" in November;

she "Glances grayly and perceives" that "All's a falling falling down" (105).

Annie's search turns frenetic as she flits wildly in the mythology of her mind, grappling for a medium to equate with the ecstasy she experienced with her lover. But comfort is not to be found in the works of the old masters, "Plato, Aeschylus, / Seneca and Mimnermus, / Pliny, Dionysius . . ." who "Lean and laugh at one who looks / To find kisses pressed in books" (106). Nor can friends help heal the pain of betrayal caused by her lover; she immerses herself in the fantasies of music and dance, the "Pirouettes" and the "Appoggiatura," to no avail, and finally, she must face her reality when "no music plays at all" (106–107). In the "inner, hasty hall" of her mind, she "Frees her lover. Drops her hands" in an act that appears to be defeat, but is the one that signals the end of her compliance in the addictive relationship with her lover, and once freed of the albatross of his presence, "Shorn and taciturn she stands," free to embark on a course of self-identification (107).

This willful act by the otherwise "late," inert, and "sweet" Annie, is her first independent act. She is admonished by the ever watchful, ever intrusive poet-narrator to think of and care for her children: "Then incline to children-dear!" (107). As though Annie needs a reminder of the devastation she has endured because of her dependency upon her lover, the poet-narrator rapidly and emphatically recalls the most destructive incidents caused by tan man's cyclonic presence in her life: the "rot and rout" of his drunken carousing with other women. Having prepared her for the startling "gust" of change she must anticipate with her lover's return home—"when the desert terrifies"—the narrator turns her attention to the weak diseased, and yet unnamed ex-soldier.

She chides tan man with the force of alliteration to tear himself away from the foreign life that has nearly destroyed him to go home: "Kill that fanged flamingo foam. Pack compunction and go home" (108). Tan man is contrite, and he is "Spent"; a mere "Skeleton" of his former self, he can only "Slide a bone beneath Her head, / Kiss Her eyes so rash and red" (107–108).

But Annie has been imbued with new strength and resilience since her lover's desertion and her own search for inner strength; she is ready to ease the pain of her lover's last days and even forgive him. By contrast, the ever judgmental poet-narrator has stripped the immoral lover of his humanness and objectified him with the designation of the relative pronoun "That," rather than the human "who."

> Pursing lips for new good-byeing
> Now she folds his rust and cough
> In the pity old and staunch.
> She remarks his feathers off;
> Feathers for such tipsy flying
> As this scarcely may re-launch
> That is dolesome and is dying. (108)

As tan man's dying is announced with the careful repetitions of "He Leaves," "Leaves," and "Leaves," as the opening words in three sequential stanzas, Annie faces the dual responsibility of rearing the "bouncy sprouts" of her impregnation as a single parent and of being responsible for facing the real world on its and her own terms (108–109). The reality of her "fate" as a Black woman in the urban ghetto of Bronzeville is visibly signaled by the absence of mythological illusions in her new world vision and the discarded lofty diction and complex word play of earlier stanzas. The matured, more cynical Annie "Who is starch or who is stone," readies herself to join the social life of the community with the "slit" eyes that recall the worldly and exotic "sleek slit-eyed gypsy" of tan man's overseas indulgence (109,104).

> Leaves his mistress to dismiss

> Memories of his kick and kiss,
> Grant her lips another smear,
> Adjust the posies at her ear,
> Quaff an extra pint of beer,
> Cross her legs upon the stool,
> Slit her eyes and find her fool. (109)

Left with only "the minuets of memory," Annie is still a young woman, rendered old by the trials and tribulations of the emotional abuse she has endured at the hands of a callous lover and her own self-delusion. In the final two stanzas of the poem, the poet-narrator reissues her reminder, now compassionate, to "Think" of Annie, who is "tweaked and twenty-four," has already passed the "green" springtime of her youth, and now faces the "hay-colored" autumn of maturity. In the final stanza, headless iambics and alliteration lure the sensibility of the reader to merge with that of the nurturing Annie, who is "almost," but not quite defeated, as she cradles the memories of her painful, but romantic illusions about her life and her lover (109).

> Think of almost thoroughly
> Derelict and dim and done.
> Stroking swallows from the sweat.
> Fingering faint violet.
> Hugging old and Sunday sun.
> Kissing in her kitchenette
> The minuets of memory. (109)

The final poem of "The Anniad," "the sonnet-ballad," is a lyrical cry for wisdom, pity, understanding, and guidance from daughter to mother. The irony is apparent as the adult Annie who has withstood the betrayal and death of a lover, the isolation, disruption, and violence of war, and faces the challenge of single parenthood, opens the poem with a question directed to the long-suffering Maxie Allen: "Oh mother, mother, where is happiness?" The repetition of the question in the final line erases the memory of the youthful tension between mother and daughter in "Maxie Allen," encloses them in a mutual circle of grief, and prefigures Annie as the emerging mother-woman of the final segment of the book, "The Womanhood," where the persistent suggestion of the stymied lives of Black women is confirmed.

Brooks' creation of the sonnet-ballad is a superb vessel for containing the deep mournful love that demands the austerity of the sonnet form, infused with the voice rhythms of the ballad for Annie's lyric cries that strain to bestow a heroic quality on her tarnished lover: "They took my lover's tallness off to war."[27] The structural regularity of the opening quatrain parallels the strict formations that define war, while the remaining quatrains suggest the folk rhythms and repetitions of balladry against the meter of the sonnet:

> He won't be coming back here any more.
> Some day the war will end, but, oh, I knew
> When he went walking grandly out that door
> That my sweet love would have to be untrue.
> Would have to be untrue. Would have to court
> Coquettish death, whose impudent and strange
> Possessive arms and beauty (of a sort)
> Can make a hard man hesitate—and change.
> And he will be the one to stammer, "Yes."
> Oh mother, mother, where is happiness? (112)

The merger of sonnet and ballad recalls Annie's compliance in her own victimization and her continued attempts to romanticize the memory of her lover. But "Coquettish death" recalls his betrayal and the sexual intrigues with the "gorgeous and gold shriek" and "maple banshee" (st. 43).

In "the sonnet-ballad," Annie reaches the threshold of

womanhood and must now forge a path to its center. As a Black, female, single parent crowded in by the ever-present racial and economic despair of America, she faces the dual tasks of surviving in a postwar climate and preparing her children to confront and survive a portentous future.

The Womanhood

The final segment of *Annie Allen* opens with a sonnet series that exhibits a continued display of expert craftsmanship, a vigorous investment in the manipulation of language, and the "sharp, black, comic irony" that Baker perceptively recognizes as a Brooks technique that sets her poetry "firmly in the black American literary tradition" (29). The ambivalent Annie who poses rhetorical questions in the first three sonnets, strengthens her mental resolve by investigating life from both social and religious perspectives and in the fourth sonnet determines that she must instruct her children on how to live as a strategy for survival.

The first three sonnets of "the children of the poor" series pose the painful questions of survival in a shifting tone of helplessness, as Annie flounders in a sea of oppression. Brooks manipulates the structures of the Petrarchan and Shakespearean forms to construct variations that illuminate Annie's quandaries. In the octave of the first sonnet, "People who have no children can be hard," the poet-narrator confronts, then quickly dismisses the childless, to focus attention on the real burden bearers: the parents. But the sestet poses a metaphoric contrast to the childless against the soft parents who are required, by the "malocclusions, the in conditions of love" to struggle for the survival of themselves and their children:

> While through a throttling darkness we others hear

> The little lifting helplessness, the queer
> Whimper-whine; whose unridiculous
> Lost softness softly makes a trap for us. (115)

The weak and anguished tone of the parents suggests failure: they can sooth but not save their children. In sonnet "2," that tone changes to one of bitter rhetorical questioning:

> What shall I give my children? who are poor,
> Who are adjudged the leastwise of the land,
> Who are my sweetest lepers, who demand
> No velvet and no velvety velour; (116)

Ambivalence is clear in the voice of the mother whose love is tinged with the hopelessness of knowing that although she has "plenitude of plan," without "access to my proper stone" to shape and direct her children's lives, not her "grief," nor her "love" are sufficient to save her "little halves" who face a dismal future.

The richness of imagery and sound in the sonnet reside in the rhetorical language, striking metaphors and rhythmic alliteration. The mother alludes to her inability to sculpture the lives of her children in "contour," "mode, design, device," and "stone," while religious language, "lepers," "graven by a hand," and "angelic," suggests a cry of despair to an indifferent God. The luxury of language in "No velvet and no velvety velour" offers stark contrast to the sparse lives of the mother and children.[28]

Ambivalence masks anger in "And shall I prime my children, pray, to pray?" The subtly vacillating tone of the poet-narrator heaps complexity on the sonnet by adopting a questioning, commanding, and finally, conciliatory point of view culminating in a line that questions the validity of religion. The initial phrase, "pray, to pray" suggests that people pray in vain for the implied justice of the American Dream, and that penitence for injustice is at best, seasonal: "Mites, come invade most frugal vestibules / Spectered with crusts of penitents' renewals / And all hysterics arrogant for a day" (117). But in the second quatrain, the anger dissipates, and the "children" are instructed: "be metaphysical mules; / Learn Lord will not distort nor leave the fray." In the sestet, the mother's confusion is apparent; she announces that she will simply wait to soothe her children when the bright light of religious disappointment blinds them: "At forehead and at fingers rather wise, / Holding the bandage ready for your eyes" (117).[29]

The turn of *Annie Allen* occurs in "The Womanhood" when the mother rises from supine helplessness to a commanding stance of would-be-warrior as a model of survival for her children. Brooks' ironic humor is evident in the octave as the mother instructs her children to "First fight. Then fiddle," and proceeds to juxtapose the elements of music into a metaphorical battleground:

> First fight. Then fiddle. Ply the slipping string
> With feathery sorcery; muzzle the note
> With hurting love; the music that they wrote
> Bewitch, bewilder. Qualify to sing
> Threadwise. (118)

The language is delightfully didactic and deceptive as the mother commands her children to use the best tools of war. Once she has admonished them to be discrete ("remote"), the ruse of fiddling is resoundingly dropped.[30] In the sestet, the voice is direct:

> But first to arms, to armor. Carry hate
> In front of you and harmony behind.
> Be deaf to music and to beauty blind.
> Win war. Rise bloody, maybe not too late
> For having first to civilize a space

Wherein to play your violin with grace. (118)

In effect, the mother has only taught her children to fight. The entire sonnet defines the initial command "First fight" with the unspoken implication that given man's predilection for war, learning to play the violin is a later, less imperative lesson.

The lesson of "First fight. Then fiddle" is the lesson of *Annie Allen.* Brooks has used all of the poetic tools at her disposal to wage a war against the injustices that assail Black Americans, with a special focus on the intimate lives of women. Tough a task as that is, it was not the only task confronting Brooks in her efforts to write *Annie Allen.* Brooks faced the 1940s dictate to write as though integration were a viable option, and that by attaining the technical skill and craftsmanship of noted white writers, she would be welcomed into the literary mainstream of America. *Annie Allen* is testament to Brooks' success on both counts. She earned the Pulitzer Prize for Poetry in 1950 as a measure of achievement for writing a book of poetry that met stringent artistic standards and reflected her social concerns, although, unlike white writers of her stature, she has yet to receive sustained critical attention. Gladys Margaret Williams makes an astute observation about the *Annie Allen* sonnet series that is applicable to the entire volume: "[Brooks] sings with full throat, communicating to the uninitiated the strains of survival upon a woman, a mother, confronted by hostile circumstances" (237).

Chapter V

The Bean Eaters (1960): Defining America

Emmett Till, a fourteen-year-old Black male from Chicago, was lynched on August 28, 1955, in Money, Mississippi, for "wolf-whistling" at a twenty-one-year-old white woman, Carolyn Bryant. While America's attention was assiduously focused on the stark journalistic headlines of national publications like *Look's* "The Shocking Story of Approved Killing in Mississippi," by William Bradford Huie, and Crisis' "Mississippi Barbarism," Gwendolyn Brooks protested poetically with a poem entitled "A Bronzeville Mother Loiters in Mississippi. Meanwhile, a Mississippi Mother Burns Bacon," and its companion piece, "The Last Quatrain of the Ballad of Emmett Till" from her third book of poetry, *The Bean Eaters* (1960)[1]. In addition to addressing the racism which is inherent in the definition of America, and by confronting the continuing reality of lynching nearly 100 years after the Emancipation Proclamation, Brooks also comments upon the equally pervasive sexism evident in the unempowered status of the Southern white woman in whose honor the deed was done. Thus, as Brooks claims Emmett Till as a member of her own cultural community of Bronzeville, by shaping a poem around his ordeal, she also defines America by its dissonant tones of blatant racism and sexism.

In *The Bean Eaters*, Brooks' voice of social consciousness takes on the sharper edge of a subtle rage as she continues to write about the Bronzeville community. And just as America is a seething caldron of social, economic, and political turbulence, so Brooks' lyrical voice sings a more cacophonic note reflective of that turbulent spirit. The decade of the fifties, radically reordered with events which would permanently redefine America and Brooks' poetry, insistently urged America towards greater social equality despite America's resistance to a quest which would seek its culmination in the full equality of all citizens. Thus in *The Bean Eaters*, Brooks' poetry is no longer limited to the vignettes of characters who people her community, nor to the day-to-day survival tactics they employ to "stay alive." As Black people in America sought to redefine their places in America and accelerate the pace of gaining social equality, so Brooks' poetry adopted a parallel tone to reflect those changes. In *The Bean Eaters*, sixteen of the thirty-six poems which capture the focus of Brooks' lyrical voice speak most clearly to the state of the racism, sexism, and classism existing in America by focusing upon the prevalence of economic deprivation, social inequality, and violence. While "A Bronzeville Mother Loiters in Mississippi. Meanwhile, a Mississippi Mother Burns Bacon" and "The Last Quatrain of the Ballad of Emmett Till" form the axle of her poetic wheel of social commentary, "The Ballad of Rudolph Reed," "The Chicago *Defender* Sends a Man to Little Rock," and "In Emanuel's Nightmare: Another Coming of Christ" function as pivotal supporting spokes. The historical backdrop pertinent to Brooks' poetry continues to fit the social and historical parameters defined by social scientists Gunnar Myrdal, Horace Cayton, St. Clair Drake, and historian Juan Williams.[2]

Just as Myrdal assesses the magnitude of the racial divisiveness which contributed to the disparate racial societies existing in America in 1944 from the perspective of a social science analysis, and Cayton and Drake map out the American strategy of segregating urban Blacks into their own American "Black Metropolis" in 1945 as a commentary on social inequality, Juan Williams also peruses the American scene, but from a different vantage point. In *Eyes on the Prize*, Williams creates a retrospective, journalistic account of the strategic events and protests which shaped the social climate of the South and in doing so, altered the face of America forever. By illuminating the individuals who made poignant contributions in nearly a decade of striving for civil rights in America, Williams chronicles *Brown* v. *the Board of Education of Topeka, Kansas* (1954), the Emmett Till lynching (1955), the Montgomery bus boycott (1955–56), the passage of the first federal Civil Rights Act since 1875 (1957), and the desegregation of Little Rock, Arkansas' Central High School (1959). Williams defines his book as an outgrowth of the television series of the same title and notes that it "chronicles these extraordinary times as a segregated America is forced, in a single decade, to take a giant step from a feudal state toward a free and open democracy" (viii).

In 1960, the urban ghetto dwellers of *The Bean Eaters* are the recast residents of Brooks' 1945 *A Street in Bronzeville*, who have been permanently altered by the venomous social confrontations of the 1950s. In their new 1960s characterizations, these segregated Bronzeville inhabitants react to the national events leading to the Civil Rights Movement and feel the tremors of Langston Hughes' "dream deferred."[3] By 1960, the Black community was manifesting the symptoms of growing, groping, and intruding upon the privileges heretofore reserved for the dominant white society, as evidenced by the topical nature of the poems in *The Bean Eaters.*

It is no wonder, then, that the publication of *The Bean Eaters* drew a near silent reception from critics for nearly three months following its debut. It was Robert H. Glauber of the *Beloit Poetry Journal* whom Brooks credits with having broken the critical silence with a "long and glowing review" of *The Bean Eaters.*[4] Other critics had been decidedly less inclined to approve Brooks' lyrical accomplishments in the face of her growing voice of social commentary. *Booklist* notes that the poems are concerned mostly with "Negroes or racial questions" and that many of them "are strong, well wrought, and broadly humanistic, but a few seem careless in technique and painfully self-conscious" (*Booklist* 650). *Bookmark* states: "Fresh, incisive verse deals with everyday situations that have disturbing undertones" (*Bookmark* 176). Frederick Bock's view of the volume is clear in his *Chicago Tribune* title, "A Prize Winning Poet Fails to Measure Up." Bock wishes that Brooks had displayed "a more controlled talent" throughout the work and feels that its "glib and smug" tone serves to "undermine" its "style and idea." But Bock's most serious charge is leveled against Brooks' "ambitious poems dealing with racial themes," specifically "A Bronzeville Mother," which he insists, "rarely becomes memorable verse." On the whole, Bock views *The Bean Eaters* as "bitterly troubled" and a testament to the fact that "the tragedy of the Negro may be simply too vast, too deep, for words" (12). Similarly, the *Virginia Kirkus'* reviewer also gives special attention to "A Bronzeville Mother," and attributes to it "savage rhythms" and comments that "if this volume does not have the same spontaneity of her first, it adds new dimensions of maturity and seriousness" (131). In Harvey Shapiro's *New York Times Book Review* of *The Bean Eaters*, he includes Brooks in his survey of poets who are responsible for the "break-up of the lyric," and states:

> The tight, self-sealed, symbolist lyric, which has been the staple of modern American verse, seems to be on the way out. The poetry replacing it . . . is a more public poetry, tied directly to the modern scene. (32)

Shapiro views the volume as basically trivial and writes: "Triteness damages the few pieces of social satire in the book" (32). Yet even given the curt critical dismissals which limit the view of the volume to a "social" work, *The Bean Eaters* is not entirely encompassed by the voice of social commentary. Though sixteen of the thirty-six poems in *The Bean Eaters* do target societal discrimination and are at best, pointed expressions of America's potential for disparate treatment of Blacks, and at worst, her tolerance of violent acts, both based purely upon race, the remaining twenty, the larger segment of the book, are self-reflective or individual ruminations on the need for all human beings to embark upon an inner struggle to meet life on its own terms. This final group of poems embodies the search for clarification of the meaning of life and emit an equally poignant note of universality in *The Bean Eaters*.

The twenty poems expressing that universality of the human spirit embody the themes of self-identification, unrequited love, and humanistic experiences. Thematically, self-identification is the target of "Strong Men, Riding Horses" and "Kid Bruin" while unrequited love is evident in "My Little 'Bout-town Gal," "For Clarice It Is Terrible Because with This He Takes Away All the Popular Songs and the Moonlights and Still Night Hushes and the Movies with Star-eyed Girls and Simpering Males," "Callie Ford," and "Priscilla Assails the Sepulcher of Love." Finally, those poems which embody themes ruminating on the human or life experience are "The Explorer," "Old Mary," "A Sunset of the City," "Pete at the Zoo," "Jack," "A Penitent Considers Another Coming of Mary," "The Contemplation of Suicide: The Temptation of Timothy," "On the Occasion of the Open-air Formation of the Olde Tymers' Walking and Nature Club," "Bessie of Bronzeville Visits Mary and Norman at a Beach-house in New Buffalo," "Naomi," "The Artists' and Models' Ball," and "The Egg Boiler."

In "Strong Men, Riding Horses," Brooks creates a sensitive portrayal of a man who clamors for self-identification based not upon a realistic role model, but upon figments of his imagination as ordered by societal stereotypes of "heroes." The would-be "hero" does not catch even a fleeting glimpse of his own strengths, so caught up is he in the film version of life. Rather, his self-image is a diminished one, consisting only of the barriers placed upon his life by normal economic constraints. He laments, "I am not like that. I pay rent, am addled / By illegible landlords, run, if robbers call." In other words, he performs as adequately as his life demands, contrary to his self-view that "I am not brave at all" (329).

Likewise, "A Sunset of the City" is a stirring depiction of aging with a dramatic use of nature which is reminiscent of Sterling Brown's "Georgia Portrait" where nature becomes the metaphor for a life entering the waning season. In "Sunset," although the first person narrator understands precisely that she is no longer "a sweet young thing" of the urban vernacular, she is very much in tune with the "happenings" of the day. The fact that she is "no longer looked at with lechery or love," is equally balanced by the fact that in her heyday she apparently was sufficiently desirable to have entertained "husband and lovers" and views their diminished ardor, though in anguish, expressed in the youthful jargon of the day, as "a real chill out" (353). Just as she has known the joy and passion of "summer," conversely she recognizes that "it is summer-gone" and with reaffirmation, "a real chill out. The fall crisp comes" (353). She claims no answers, but admits to a "dual dilemma" awaiting her in a future in "this cold house" or alternatively the option "to leap and die" (354). Her strength and resilience are evident in her closing lines, which do not lament, but hint at a curiosity which will be her guiding force in old age. She queries: "Somebody muffed it? Somebody wanted to joke" (354).

As evident in this series of brief explications, there is as much variety of subject matter in *The Bean Eaters* as there was in Brooks' 1945 *A Street in Bronzeville.* To that point, George Kent aptly notes that "the universe of *The Bean Eaters* is a very complicated one," and yet the variety of issues addressed represents "numerous balances" as they touch upon "the racial and intraracial; the social and metaphysical; the individual and the group" (*Life* 146). The reality is that Brooks' more focused attention on the issues of racial disparities and social injustices confronting America mirrors what was actually occurring at the time. In interviews with Paul Angle (1967) and George Stavros (1969), she addresses the issue of her social voice. Angle queries: "Is the poet affected by today's social unrest?" Brooks responds:

> The poet, first and foremost an individual with a personal vision, is also a member of society. What affects society affects a poet. So I, starting out, *usually* in the grip of a high and private suffusion, may find by the time I have arrived at a last line that there is quite some public clamor in my product. (*RPO* 138)

Stavros makes a pointed inquiry: "Do you feel, as some readers of yours have said, that your own poetry has abandoned its lyrical simplicity for an angrier, more polemical public voice?" Brooks responds:

> No, I have not abandoned beauty, or lyricism, and I don't consider myself a polemical poet. I'm a black poet, and I write about what I see, what interests me, and I'm seeing new things. Many things that I'm seeing now I was blind to before, but I don't sit down at the table and say, 'Lyricism is out." No, I just continue to write about what confronts me. (*RPO* 151)

Thus, although Brooks disclaims any intention of "writing poems with the *idea* that they are to become 'social forces,'" the reality is that by way of defining the urban landscape of Bronzeville in the social climate leading to her 1960 publication, Brooks was also defining America by way of its violent relationship with Black people (*RPO* 153).

Brooks defines America from the vantage point of the urban landscape she paints in *A Street in Bronzeville*, expands upon it in *Annie Allen*, and clearly delineates in a message of social commentary in *The Bean Eaters*. To construct a realistic and identifiable blueprint of urban Black life in Bronzeville, Brooks introduces the personae who inhabit this cultural milieu, conveys the conditions to which Black Americans are subjected, depicts the survival tactics they employ, and finally, delves into the intimacies and intricacies within which they exist, by creating a series of character vignettes. In *A Street in Bronzeville* poems like "kitchenette building," "the mother," and the "Hattie Scott" series, the racial segregation and economic disparity of the Black community are evident. Similarly in *Annie Allen*, the community is depicted in themes of racial entrapment evident in "birth in a narrow room," "downtown vaudeville," and "Beverly Hills, Chicago." By contrast, in *The Bean Eaters* Brooks looks at the same urban landscape, but from a more socially informed perspective than is evident in her earlier works. Where *A Street in Bronzeville* massages the message of social commentary by embedding it in layers of poetic technique, complex stanzaic patterns, and myriad metrical structures; and the social context of *Annie Allen* is all but obscured by the same factors, as well as complex allusions and mythological and classical references; it is *The Bean Eaters* that breaks the binds of poetic confinement to deliver a succinct message, by a recognizable blend of free verse, sonnets, and ballads, of the exclusion of Black people from real freedom and equality in America.

In addition to the poetic commentaries on the prevalence of economic deprivation, social inequality, and violence perpetrated upon the Black community, *The Bean Eaters* also poses weighty propositions on gender and class distinctions which, though specifically informed by the Bronzeville community, also have application to society at large. In the poems, "Mrs. Small," "Jesse Mitchell's Mother," "A Man of the Middle Class," and "The Ghost at the Quincy Club," Brooks creates portrayals of the conflicts of sexism and classism in America. As an apt representation, the diminished mental, occupational, and gender status of Mrs. Small is metaphorically defined in the diminutive pronouncement of her name; likewise, where her husband becomes personalized and individualized by the introduction of his first name, "Jim," Mrs. Small's impersonal identifiers as woman and wife yield her no individual importance in the world. Rather Mrs. Small's character is further reduced by her "peculiar look . . . with the half-open mouth and the half-mad eyes / And the smile half-human." The site of Mrs. Small's female domain is a strategic confinement to the kitchen, and her brief excursions to the front door result in her confusion, "mistake[s]," and "Apologies."

Mrs. Small's worldly contributions are gender-related and relegated to her "small" domestic sphere as signified by the location of her personal belongings aligned with the domestic tools in the kitchen:

> And the coffee pot.
> Pocketbook. Pot
> Pot. Pocketbook. (341)

She clings to the coffee pot and to the idea of concocting an apple pie as the last vestiges of her precarious sanity. Her sole identifiers, wife to Jim and mother to a rowdy brood of ten, permit her demeanor to collapse when she is challenged by the task of interacting with someone alien to the realm of her daily existence. Because her husband has aligned her value with her ability to make "the best coffee in town," it seems appropriate to Mrs. Small to carry the tool of her trade, the coffee pot, to the front door as she conducts "business" (343). Her sad reality is that her individuality has been subsumed by her family identification, and domesticity is the sole arena of the "world's business" as she is privy to it (343). By commenting upon the constricted existence of Mrs. Small, Brooks paints a portrait of the potentially limiting role of women as wives and mothers and the diminished stature often accorded them both by society at large and their own self-images.

In "Jessie Mitchell's Mother," Brooks again ventures into the women's domicile, this time by exploring a mother-daughter relationship further complicated by the ongoing intraracial color tensions which have permeated the Black community since the days of slavery. One of the most vigorously resisted yet visible realities of miscegenation, the subtle color nuances which make up the varying skin colorations of Black Americans, or the "Black-and-Tan Motif," as labeled by Arthur P. Davis, produces an even greater conflict in a power struggle between a weak and dying light-skinned mother and her darker daughter. Metaphorically, the "yellow rag that was Jessie Mitchell's mother" views her "Young, and so thin, and so straight" daughter and finds perverse comfort in the notion that her daughter's future promises to be "black, and jerkier" as a societal parallel to the daughter's skin color, versus the mother's own "exquisite yellow youth" (345). Perched upon the seemingly safe pedestal of color superiority, the mother nevertheless grudgingly and ironically admires her Black daughter, who, though not the "lemon-hued lynx" of "the ballad of chocolate Mabbie" (*A Street in Bronzeville* 30), possesses something more precious and enduring—a posture "So straight! as if nothing could ever bend her" (344).

Further evidence of the still raging color conflict recently received new voice in film version at the hands of producer, director Spike Lee. In his movie *School Daze*, Lee creates a fictitious portrayal of intraracial color conflicts on Black American college campuses. And there is a painful childhood rhyme that is well known in urban Black neighborhoods and provides a succinct commentary on the intraracial color conflict:

> If you're *white*, you're right;
> If you're *yellow*, you're mellow;
> If you're *brown*, you can hang around

But, if you're *black*, stand back! (Davis 90)

By commenting upon the intraracial color conflict in the seemingly unusual terrain of familial relationships, Brooks' narrator offers a brief but sad commentary on how far Black America has wandered into the realm of racial prejudices, dictated by skin color and initiated by the dominant white society. Thus, the near hatred Jessie's mother feels for the daughter, spawned by her own mixed blood, is a testament to the stereotypes created by whites to view Blacks based upon skin color differences and adapted by Blacks to construct racial barriers within their own communities.

Closely aligned to these poems offering social commentary in the women's sphere and intraracial conflicts are poems depicting situations involving classism. Both "A Man of the Middle Class" and "The Ghost at the Quincy Club" fit into this category. The title of the latter poem offers an ironic play on the word "ghost" which references the original white occupants as well as the residual memories of the more lavish lifestyles once housed in an exclusive "club" setting. The poem also provides visual imagery which highlights the extent to which the community of Bronzeville has undergone racial transition as integration has left its footprints in the wake of a rapid exodus of whites to distant suburban areas and the influx of poor Blacks into the remaining tenement dwellings and rooming houses made from older mansions. In *The Women of Brewster Place* (1982), Gloria Naylor offers a historical overview of how integration occurs in declining urban areas already ravaged by several generations of immigrants. On the threshold of squalor and decay, the reality of Brewster Place's "third generation of children who drifted into the block and precipitated the exodus of the remaining Mediterraneans" may also be applicable to the residents of the Quincy Club (4). Additionally, the poem recalls Wright's depiction of Chicago in his novel *Native Son* (1940) and the "spacious white neighborhoods" bordering the teeming ghettoes. Wright's protagonist, Bigger Thomas, a Black youth from an adjacent tenement area which threatens to overtake the nearby white mansions and "Quincy Clubs," views the white area and thinks, "This was a cold and distant world; a world of white secrets carefully guarded" (45).

Brooks' first stanza, in terse trimeter, invites a vision of the ghostly characterization of Wright's blind Mrs. Dalton, who "wafts" through the corridors and down the halls of the family mansion, which sits at 4605 S. Drexel Boulevard in pre-Bronzeville days. She is "a tall, thin, white woman, walking silently, her hands lifted delicately in the air and touching the walls to either side of her" (47) who nearly parallels the persona in Brooks' opening lines, "All filmy down she drifts / In filmy stuffs and all" which confirms the same character profile (359). The concept of wealth and old money is introduced in Brooks' emphatic line, "This was a mansion once!—" and expanded upon in stanza two where the differences between the elite of the "velvet voices" of former occupancy, versus the lower class folk of the "raucous Howdys" of current occupancy are evident (359). Similarly, Naylor notes that the new residents of Brewster Place "had their own language and music and codes" (2).

"The Ghost at the Quincy Club" is a commentary on the effects of social change through the acquisition of urban ghettoes by Blacks and the resultant class issues involved. Thus, Wright's Mrs. Dalton who already "had millions when [Mr. Dalton] married her" (57) and created even more wealth, could be one of the "daughters-of-gentlemen" of the poem (359). By contrast, the closing mismatched couplet of Brooks' poem suggests a less than a parallel existence of the former and current residents:

> Where Tea and Father were (each clear
> And lemony) are dark folk, drinking beer. (359)

The ironic implications suggested by the tetrameter of the first line and pentameter of the second line offer an inverse closing portrait of the impending social change. The use of the short tetrameter line, familiarly associated with popular ballad lines and the rollicking naturalness of common folk, here reverses itself to represent the more genteel elements of the poem. Conversely, the often solemn pentameter line, chiefly noted for its historical association with weighty, austere subject matter, here inclines toward the common folk who are taking up residence in the mansion. The narrator's sardonic perspective is subtly infused in the regularity of the tetrameter line, versus the irregular pentameter line, and slowed down by the spondee, which highlights the incongruity of "dark folk, drinking beer" at the Quincy Club.

Similarly, "A Man of the Middle Class" symbolizes the strivings of some Bronzevillians which may culminate in upward mobility but with more dire results than expected given the illusion of perfection often perpetrated in the portrayal of the American Dream. The first-person narrator defines America based upon his exposure to middle-class lifestyle of the dominant white society and the resulting confusion he experiences. Unlike Satin-Legs in "The Sundays of Satin-Legs Smith" (26–31), who not only does not hanker to improve his conditions by leaving his Black community, but is also unaware that his ghetto lifestyle is less desirable than any other, the narrator in "A Man of the Middle Class" knows exactly what has been withheld from him as a Black man in an urban ghetto and has sought to correct his deprivation by ambitiously pursuing the American Dream. Upon his return to Bronzeville, following an abortive career endeavor, he realizes that his venture into the land of middle-class status was not without its new and different discomforts. When he states, "I'm what has gone out blithely and with noise / Returning!" he is admitting to the ills which confronted him in the life of "the rich and famous," which from afar, appeared to be immensely gratifying. He is "bedraggled" and limps "laxly" with an "Uncomely trudge" (355).

Ultimately, what he sought out he captured; yet the "antique firearms. Blackamoors. Chinese / Rugs. Ivories. / Bronzes. Everything I Wanted" are insufficient for him (356). His "know-nows" (Brooks, *RPO* 45) come from "the executives [he] copied long ago, / The ones who, forfeiting Vicks salve, Prayer book and Mother, shot themselves last Sunday." Now that he knows that life's most precious gifts are in life itself and not in the material successes of "architectural" gardens, "canvas walls," "flowers in vases," "Bizarre prints," or "odoriferous furs," he is finally privy to the real-life secrets of "Giants" whose material successes do not yield them any real happiness (356). Though his original goal was to rise above Bronzeville and lead "the good life," the narrator is forced to admit that in order to "do better" and "get ahead," he must forfeit the folkways that are important to his life and his culture; and finally, he is still without a viable direction for the future. In short, the class issue addressed in the two poems suggests, in "The Ghost of the Quincy Club," that though integration is accompanied by a lower socioeconomic status which forces these new tenement dwellers to survive on the perimeter of poverty, there is also a vibrancy for living that yields them staying power in the face of that poverty. And, in "A Man of the Middle Class," Black folks who have elevated their material existence, moved away and adopted the cultural nuances of whites ultimately "limp laxly" in the discomfiture of an alien culture and finally seek solace by returning home to Bronzeville and their own culture.

The undertone of poverty in this community of "bean eaters," which takes on the ambiance of class issues in the above two poems, flatly announces itself as economic deprivation in the poems "The Bean Eaters," "The Crazy Woman," and "A Lovely Love." Unlike the note of flippancy expressed by Langston Hughes' personae in "Ennui":

> It's such a
> bore
> Being always
> Poor. (*Selected Poems* 131)

Brooks' depictions exude a note of melancholy over the fate of the ghetto dwellers:

> Two who are Mostly Good.
> Two who have lived their day,
> But keep on putting on their clothes
> And putting things away. (330)

Though "The Bean Eaters" is an apt portrayal of aging, as characterized by "this old yellow pair," it is also a social commentary on the dire poverty which has afflicted their lives in which home ownership, a goal of the American Dream, is not a genuine option for them; even in old age they have, not an apartment, but merely a "rented back room." The title poem of the book, *The Bean Eaters* is no casual romanticized reference to the aging of one Black couple; it is the report on the socioeconomic status of an entire Black community, evident in the opening quatrain:

> They eat beans mostly, this old yellow pair.
> Dinner is a casual affair.
> Plain chipware on a plain and creaking wood,
> Tin flatware. (330)

The beans eaten by this couple replicate the beans eaten by an entire community and are indicative of the meager economic resources of that community. The "Plain chipware on a plain and creaking wood, / Tin flatware" are the evidences of an entire life of "beans in their rented back room," while the memories of "with twinklings and twinges" admit to the joys, as well as sorrows of a life closing out with only "beads and receipts and dolls and cloths, / tobacco crumbs, vases and fringes" (330). By creating a vacillating metrical pattern, Brooks aligns the uneven economic straits of the couple's life to the formal structure of the poem. In the opening quatrain, she alternates the pentameter of the first and third lines with the tetrameter and trimeter of the second and fourth lines, followed by varied tetrameter and trimeter lines in the second quatrain. The final free verse stanza sprawls into uneven lines, enhanced by the rhetorical devices of anadiplosis and alliteration, and culminating in a catalogue of salvaged items "And remembering / Remembering" (330).

Likewise in "The Crazy Woman," poverty is the underlying theme, though somewhat camouflaged in the symbolism of nature. The crazy woman refuses to sing in May because her song does not parallel the rites of spring, rebirth and regeneration, for which that month is known. Symbolically, she will however, sing in bleak, damp, and cold November whose "frosty dark" matches her own depressed economic condition. Her "song of gray" recalls the "kitchenette building" of *A Street in Bronzeville* where the residents are "Grayed in, and gray," and dreams are not expected to survive the "onion fumes" (20). The first-person narrator plays on the oxymoron "sing most terribly" to stress the cognizance of the crazy woman who, in understanding that "A May song should be gay," will, appropriately, sing her song of life in wintry November (360). Ironically, her shrewd awareness that the song of ghetto dwellers should be situated not in May, but in November, makes her, perhaps, not so crazy at all.

And third, in the trilogy of poems on economic deprivation, the narrator of "A Lovely Love" makes strident attempts, by way of the sonnet form, to sing of love, yet only manages to evoke a sad, wistful poem of urgency due to the pervasiveness of poverty. This sonnet of sullied love makes a pretense of striving for the grandeur of the Shakespearean sonnet, both in form and content, while simultaneously acknowledging each of the things which prohibit its subject from attaining the heights of pure love. The sonnet addresses urban poverty in its allusions to "alleys," "a hall," and "stairways" as the boudoirs of love, rather than more elevated places of intimacy (363). Additionally, the epithets of the janitor "cheapen" what might otherwise be "hyacinth darkness" to mere "rot" while the harsh sounding words "splintery," "thrown," and "scraped," serve to support the rough conditions under which the lovers must pursue their attempts at "a lovely love."

The "rot" of this old and decaying tenement dwelling (which also informs "The Lovers of the Poor" where "The stench; the urine, cabbage, and dead beans" contribute to the "squalor") is not to be confused with the rot of adjacent white areas of the city, like "Beverly Hills, Chicago" where: "The summer ripeness rots. But not raggedly" (*Annie Allen* 128). And just as the meaning of "rot" is altered in this urban arena, so the message of the final quatrain falls short of its ideal goal of comparison:

> That is the birthright of our lovely love
> In swaddling clothes. Not like that Other one.
> Not lit by any fondling star above.
> Not found by any wise men, either. Run. (363)

The lovers are not permitted the ethereal meaning accorded the two celestial figures of the barn, nor will men come bearing gifts from afar. In fact, since the lovers are trespassing, they must exit before they are caught and punished. Finally, in the closing couplet, the young couple yield to the reality of their environment and the fact that the allusion to a higher religious birth is not to be their own:

> People are coming. They must not catch us here
> Definitionless in this strict atmosphere. (363)

Expanding the inherent theme of economic deprivation, *The Bean Eaters* also contains four poems which provide direct commentary on the parallel and pervasive cloud of social inequality that hovers over the urban, Black community of Bronzeville, emitting the deadly fumes of hopelessness and despair. That social inequality exacts its toll in the failure of young men to emerge educationally prepared to pursue higher economic goals, poverty-stricken tenement dwellers to rise above the enforced residential segregation of their lives, and workers to become gainfully employed in the face of reductively explicit negative racial stereotypes, born in the era of slavery, which label them "subhuman" and thus limit them to the lowest economic strata of society. The poems "We Real Cool," "The Lovers of the Poor," "Bronzeville Man with a Belt in the Back," and "Bronzeville Woman in a Red Hat," signal the plight of Black Americans who are entrapped in the all-Black community of Bronzeville, by employing the kind of irony and understatement which address the stoicism of the residents and afford some wry humor directed at the perpetrators of racism.

The pre-rap style of "We Real Cool" is immediately offset by the use of the urban vernacular which identifies these young men, by virtue of having "left school," as unlikely candidates for assimilation into the dominant white society and thus sharing in the economic gains which might otherwise be available to them. And because they tell us that "We real cool," one might be tempted to buy into a devil-may-care attitude on their part which would then, of course, make them fully cognizant of and totally responsible for their own plight. Yet because *A Street in Bronzeville* has paved the way for detecting the innate racism in their definition, the control these young men have over their destiny is, at best, questionable.

In "Gwendolyn the Terrible: Propositions on Eleven Poems," Hortense Spillers duly notes that Brooks is "deliberately subverting the romance of sociological pathos." Similarly, Gary Smith, in "Brooks' 'We Real Cool,'" suggests that the otherwise romantic undertone of carousing and drunken revelry as espoused by the reference to the bacchius three-syllable foot metrics, a definitive expression of the ancient Roman religious tributes to Bacchus, the mythological god of wine, is countered in Brooks' use of the "rare *antibacchius* metrical pattern" (49). Though both of these observations are correct, and as Smith posits, "the meter counters the *carpe diem* theme in the poem and deflates the spirit of cool adventure," the poem tells even more, given the implications of its historical referents (49).

Melhem defines the "coolness" of the "children['s]" behavior as a bravado display of their "peer-group sense of stylish behavior," a theory which, on the surface, might be acceptable, but for the overall lack of control of individual and collective destinies in the community at large (129). In Melhem's assessment:

> the pool players defend themselves against defeat, despair, and indifference by rejecting social norms. Their "coolness" of alienation responds by dropping out, drinking, debauching, dying. It is this wasteful aggression against the self, this fragile wall of bravado that the poet mourns. (129)

While Melhem's assessment is insightful in its definitive explication of the symptoms of hopelessness and despair, it clearly invites a probe into the causal nature of these symptoms. Several literary genres depict apt situations that under close scrutiny cast a revealing glare on the origins and manifestations of these symptoms.

In Wright's *Native Son*, protagonist Bigger Thomas grapples with myriad elements of urban dwelling, uppermost among them, "fear," along with a machismo bravado and a thuggish persona in an attempt to survive in Bronzeville. Bigger and his poolroom cohorts have surrendered to the pressures of poverty, segregation, and discrimination by dropping out of school, bereft of a viable means of survival. Thus, Bigger daily deliberates over whether or not he should visit what Drake and Cayton in *Black Metropolis* define as one of the "centers of activity" in Bronzeville, the poolroom, to talk and hang out with his buddies (381). To wit, Brooks' "of De Witt Williams on his way to Lincoln Cemetery," is a final view of a funeral procession which must drive the dead man "past the Pool Hall" as a part of the last rites accorded one who has spent his life on the streets of Bronzeville (*A Street in Bronzeville* 39).

In a nearly parallel comparison of the protagonists of "We Real Cool," the educational deficiencies of Wright's characters prohibit them from pursuing positions requiring technical skill or a strong academic aptitude. Thus, although this group also spends their days lurking in and about Doc's Poolroom, much like the seven pool players in "We Real Cool," far from being content with a veneer of "coolness," these men of limited options and aspirations and exaggerated fears watch airplanes soar, only to admit to the futility of ever being privileged enough to attend aviation school. And even if they were to reach a true level of professional accomplishment, Ralph Ellison's Todd in "Flying Home" provides crucial evidence of the consternation of ever attaining social equality even when one does matriculate with the proper credentials.

The state of racial segregation and discrimination in urban Black communities like Bronzeville is made patently clear in Myrdal's chapters on "social inequality." What the sparse lines of the poem do not state overtly, but do convey implicitly, is that "the pool players" are identifiable as a part of a larger urban contingency of Black people living in "forced segregation" and suffering in "cultural isolation" (574). Thus, the Black men of Bronzeville are not to be taken merely as "pool players," but as metaphorically indicative of the long term effects of segregation on Black Americans who are entrapped within the confines of their own poverty-stricken communities and ostracized, based upon negative racial stereotypes of the dominant white society. The pool players fit Myrdal's description of Northern Negroes:

"wherever Negroes lived in insignificant numbers they met considerable social segregation and discrimination" (599).

In "We Real Cool," Brooks, in four couplets systematically arranged in monosyllabics, paints a terse picture of the streets of Bronzeville and some of its daily inhabitants in a "fat-less" stanzaic style Madhubuti attributes only to her post-1967 work (preface *RPO* 22).

> We real cool. We
> Left school. We
>
> Lurk late. We
> Strike straight. We
>
> Sing sin. We
> Thin gin. We
>
> Jazz June. We
> Die soon. (331)

The overriding tone of the poem is the fear which emanates from the communal chant of "We." The terminal caesura leading to enjambed lines suggests a hesitancy—what Brooks terms their "basic uncertainty"—rather than a note of finality in the first person monologue, for youths whose comfort level is in peer support versus a heightened individuality (*RPO* 156). Paradoxically, the speaker touts his ability to veer from societal norms, but finally must admit that he needs the group to forge a new trail, as confirmed by the communal definition inherent in the opening epigraph:

> The pool players.
> Seven at the golden shovel. (331)

Brooks' precise wordplay makes it manifestly clear that the pool players are not merely "loitering" outside the pool hall, but that they "Lurk late" with the ominous overtones indicative of impending furtive actions or movements. In a need to confront and distort societal norms within their proscribed space, they proudly declare that they "Strike straight" in a duplicity of meaning denoting their success as pool sharks and applying that same skill to hit their human marks as they violently "Jazz June" and in an act of divine reciprocity, "Die soon."

Like "We Real Cool," "The Lovers of the Poor" engages the theme of social inequality which is the underlying reality of the economic deprivation of Bronzeville. However, unlike the laconic stanzaic form and meter of the former poem, "The Lovers of the Poor" embraces a sprawling free verse form indicative of the seemingly boundless good will of the uneasy philanthropers. The third-person omniscient narrator vacillates from a purely reportorial style, emanating from the scene of the action, to an editorial stance to expose the polarized lifestyles of the poor versus their "betters."

The most striking feature of this seven-stanza poem is the use of repetition, especially alliteration, to portray the redundancy in the lives of the poor and to signal how rapidly the rich can tire of the tedium of subsidizing the poverty stricken. Because these ladies "Who are full, / Sleek, tender-clad, fit, fiftyish, a-glow, all" are so busy idealizing the plight of "The worthy poor. The very very worthy / And beautiful poor," they do not immediately notice that the poor are "Perhaps just not too swarthy? / Perhaps just not too dirty. . ." (350). Rather they would prefer "something less than derelict or dull." In truth, "The Lovers of the Poor . . . The Ladies from the Ladies' Betterment League . . . [whose] guild is giving money to the poor . . . allotting largesse to the Lost," have tired very quickly of these "noxious needy ones," whose lives amid the stench, dirt, and "*general* oldness" are too far removed from their own "delicate rose-finger[ed]" suburban lives to be comprehended or tolerated:

Keeping their scented bodies in the center
Of the hall as they walk down the hysterical hall,
They allow their lovely skirts to graze no wall,
Are off at what they manage of a canter,
And, resuming all the clues of what they were,
Try to avoid inhaling the laden air. (352)

Thus, in order to escape the dirt, darkness, oldness, and stench of this stale tenement, the ladies must "achieve the outer air," "hie," "canter" to the comfortable refuge of their Lake Forest and Glencoe habitats (352).

In "The Lovers of the Poor," Brooks recaptures and enlarges the lens used in *A Street in Bronzeville* which thus renders those poems, not simple character vignettes, but works of social commentary encompassing the themes of the economic deprivation, social inequality, segregation, and discrimination evident in the urban Black community. The tenement of "The Lovers of the Poor" enlarges the portrait of prudent poverty evident in "The Bean Eaters," while "the tumbling children" sharply contrasts with the "silence" of the unborn children in "the mother" (21); likewise, the material wealth of the ladies who "walk down the "hysterical hall," encased in the aura of their "Spode, Lowestoft, [and] candelabra," recall the absence "of baroque, / Rococo" in "Satin Legs-Smith," who duly substitutes his "hysterical ties" for real wealth (44).

The issue of social inequality, though also prevalent in "Bronzeville Man with a Belt in the Back," does not share an overt affiliation with the gloomy pall of economic deprivation casting a cloud over the above mentioned poems. Instead, "Bronzeville Man" evokes the spirit of Melhem's "heroic possibility in ordinary life" by its heroic tone and subtle allusions to knighthood (136). The repetition of the initial line of the opening stanza in the solitary closing line, "In such an armor he may rise and raid," and "In such an armor he cannot be slain," provide formal protective enclosure for this knight of the ghetto who is "unafraid," wields an "able sword," and "slice[s] the shadows . . . hashing them down" (362).

The reader is informed by the knowledgeable third-person narrator that the conditions of life in Bronzeville are such that one must always be prepared to fight for one's very existence. "Bronzeville Man," then, is duly prepared for his anonymous enemies with the outer accouterments of weaponry and the inner protectiveness of his "good broad nonchalance" and "an airiness." Yet there is still an implied danger and a potential for violence in his movements as he reserves his rampages in "The dark cave" for "after midnight." The shadows he must destroy, in order to reap the accolades of the "gasping crowd," are reflective of the obstacles one faces in the urban ghetto of Bronzeville and the need for men to fight for their survival as role models for the rest of the community. His successful survival stands to earn him the "praises" and "love" of his community, for which he searches (362).

"Bronzeville Woman in a Red Hat" once again returns to the theme of economic deprivation as an adjunct to social inequality as evidenced by the subheading "Hires out to Mrs. Miles" which not only distances the domestic servant from her "wage-paying mistress," but further establishes her lack of importance and parallel lack of individual identity (367). Though the title vaguely references any Bronzeville woman, it paradoxically limits and distinguishes this particular woman by its allusion to her "red hat." The symbolism inherent in the ironic referral to her red hat provides an alternative view of a Black woman as a domestic, versus one whose private life speaks to more vibrant, independent, and sassy inclinations. Like Hattie Scott, in "the end of the day" and "at the hair-dressers" (*A Street in Bronzeville* 51, 53), the woman's red hat signals a well-established life counterpoised against the financial and physical constraints of life as a domestic.

The radiant energy innate to the meaning of red is also apparent in poems by both Langston Hughes and Sterling

Brown. In "When Sue Wears Red," Hughes hails Susanna Jones whose red dress is indicative of her "beauty," while in "To Sallie, Walking," Brown similarly complements the "vividness" of Sallie, who, when she walks, is "provocative, discreet." Yet ultimately, by contrast, this same "red," suggestive of vibrant life, will eventually inform the violence of lynching in "A Bronzeville Mother" and "The Last Quatrain of the Ballad of Emmett Till."

The menial domestic role of the Bronzeville woman is a role that has been common to working class Black women, both in the South, since the days of slavery, and in the North, since the days of the Great Migration. Brooks' use of free verse and a random line structure addresses the lack of rhyme or reason in Mrs. Miles' first attributing the animalistic traits of "A lion, really. Poised / To pounce. A Puma. A panther. A black / Bear," to a human being then, though ambivalent, entrusting the care of "her creamy child" to such a "creature" (367). The first verse pointedly signifies the woman as subhuman in the lines, "They had never had one in the house before," and "There it stood in the door" (367). And rather than concede to the attractiveness of the red hat, which is clearly informed by an unfamiliar culture, Mrs. Miles labels the hat "rash, but refreshing— / In a tasteless way, of course." She is duly offended by the "dull dare, / The semi-assault of that extraordinary blackness" of her "slave" (367).

The second verse of the two-part poem permits a recognition of the fact that Mrs. Miles' seemingly disparate racial views are not limited to Black people, but a dual statement on racism and classism, since she holds a diminished view of her Irish housekeeper's humanity as well. Though Patsy Houlihan's absenteeism is a result of the tragic events surrounding the murder of her daughter, that fact countenances no sympathy on the part of "mistress" Miles. Instead, her need for "the biscuit blending," "the curry," "soup," and "tossed salad" steer her thoughts to Mrs. Houlihan's inconsiderate ways, but not to her own inhumanity. Grammatically, the Black maid is labeled a nonhuman entity in the final lines of part I:

> The Alert Agency had leafed through its files—
> On short notice could offer
> Only this dusky duffer
> That now made its way to her kitchen and sat on her
> kitchen stool. (369)

The references to her as "that" and "it," rather than the human "who," set the stage with a backdrop for Mrs. Miles' horror at having a "beast," not a person, kiss her white child, whose finger is bleeding and who longs for some "human humoring" (369).

But ironically, the white child's affinity for the Black maid, far from being the world-shaking event which defines his mother's reaction, is for him a show of affection in a world otherwise peopled by his mother, whom the Irish woman labels "'Inhuman.' And 'a fool.' / And 'a cool One.'" Though Mrs. Miles is filled with "disgust" at the intimacy of the act and senses that she has been deprived of a valuable possession, which she tries to extricate or "pry the ordure from the cream," the child resists with an emphatic "No," and "Kissed back the colored maid" after becoming "Conscious of kindness, easy creature bond" (369).

Brooks' poem recalls a similar scenario in Ann Petry's *The Street* (1946). The poverty-stricken protagonist, Lutie Johnson, notes in this stream-of-consciousness narrative that "she'd cleaned another woman's house and looked after another woman's child while her own marriage went to pot . . . " (30). Indeed, in a contextual structure nearly parallel to "Bronzeville Woman in a Red Hat," Lutie arrives at the interview for a domestic position in "high-heeled shoes and thin stockings and this wide-brimmed hat" quite in contrast to the "ribbed stockings made of very fine cotton and flat-heeled moccasins. . . and no hat" of her mistress-to-be (36). Similarly, Lutie is placed in charge of a white child who was "just a nice, happy kid, liking her at once, always wanting to be with her" (39). And the same "coolness" evident in the character of Mrs. Miles, likewise frames the profile of Lutie's mistress: "She wasn't too sure that Mrs. Chandler was over fond of Little Henry; she never held him on her lap or picked him up and cuddled him the way mothers do their children. She was always pushing him away from her" (39).

This close bond between Black domestic workers and the white children they tended is the focus of an article, "Say Dixie Whites Are Not Bad Folks," by Lew Sadler. As he elucidates some of the social norms and the "good neighbor" codes existing between Southern Blacks and whites, Sadler highlights discernible evidence of Blacks in the lives of whites:

> My wife was raised by a Negro woman, as have so many other ladies of the south. That still is the case. You can drive by our parks and yards and see how many white children are cared for by, not white nurses, but colored women . . .
>
> I've seen many times the mother come home from work, and the kids would hold on to the Negro woman's legs letting themselves be dragged to the sidewalk and on into the car before letting go, because they didn't want her to leave. Does that look like we are allergic to Negroes? (Williams 55)

Sadler's perspective establishes the Southern origins of the Black woman as primary caretaker to the white child and recalls the days of slavery when, among many domestic roles the Black woman held, nurturing her mistress' children was deemed more critical than caring for her own. Thus, although the poem suggests a Northern environment, it also recalls the transmission of the Southern social codes, which were transplanted along with the Southern Blacks who migrated north in hopes of social equality.[5]

The lack of humanity accorded Black Americans, as depicted in the poem, "Bronzeville Woman in a Red Hat," is also reflective of America's persistent predilection for violence where Blacks are concerned. As Brooks' voice urges toward the political in the poem "In Emanuel's Nightmare: Another Coming of Christ," the allusion to violence, though subtle, is distinctly evident in terms of defining America. A historical perspective of the social climate of the years 1945–1960, the period covered by Brooks' first three works, bears out white America's abiding potential for violence, directed at both their fellow Black citizens at home, as well as their engagements in World War I and World War II.

"Emanuel's Nightmare," a social commentary embedded in a dramatic monologue, addresses the need for humans to involve themselves in war even when the option for peace is a viable one. Brooks' superb use of repetition and polyptoton carry off the tone of inquiry coupled with sarcasm as the speaker embarks upon a meticulous examination of the peoples' choices. In the first of a series of blank verse stanzas, the speaker establishes the polar opposites of war and peace in the repetition of "quiet" and "noise" (383). Formally, in its first stanza, the poem signals the strict alignment of troops marching to battle. The redundant iambic pentameter, which is akin to the drone of impending war, is a persistent refrain throughout the poem.

The very ideology of peace offered in the opening stanza, "The sleepy sun sat on us, and those clouds / Dragged dreamily. Well, it was interesting—," is ultimately rejected in the final stanza, where the speaker asserts, "The people wanted war. War's in their hearts" (385). Striving towards this final determination, Brooks' speaker artfully weaves religious subterfuge to suggest that humans really do not advocate harmony at all. Thus it is war, and not the "creed" of "freedom and justice for all," that rules the world. Even as the women think that "'The Judgement Day has come,'" they violently knock "each other down." And though the speaker expresses sheer adoration of "God's son" who "had come down, He said, to clean the earth / Of the dirtiness of war," he finally acknowledges the "human aim" for war, and not peace (385).

The fact that Brooks ends *The Bean Eaters* with "In Emanuel's Nightmare: Another Coming of Christ" is significant because of the ongoing racial turmoil in America, often running concurrently with large scale wars abroad. Poetically, she expresses a pivotal sentiment of many Americans, which is the ironic question of the importance of religion in a world focused upon violence.

"A Bronzeville Mother Loiters in Mississippi. Meanwhile, a Mississippi Mother Burns Bacon"

The most explicit poems of social commentary in *The Bean Eaters*, "A Bronzeville Mother Loiters in Mississippi. Meanwhile, a Mississippi Mother Burns Bacon," "The Last Quatrain of the Ballad of Emmett Till," "The Chicago *Defender* Sends a Man to Little Rock," and "The Ballad of Rudolph Reed," reflect the ongoing pattern of discrimination and racial violence in America, even as America gropes for social equality. Thematically, these poems individualize acts of violence and lynching and extend themselves even further as they explore the psychological ramifications on the presiding heroes and heroines. Historically, John Hope Franklin examines the prevalence of lynching in the United States and presents the results in his seminal work on African American history, *From Slavery to Freedom* (1947). During the last sixteen years of the nineteenth century, the South could boast of over 2,500 lynchings and by the outbreak of World War I, over 1,000 more had occurred. The persistence of violence targeted at Blacks in the South was especially extreme in Alabama, Georgia, and Louisiana, where lynching statistics were the highest in the nation. Franklin's work also clarifies the misconception that most Blacks had been lynched for raping white women. The reality is that most lynchings were the result of robberies, insults to whites, and other minor offenses. Yet, as Franklin states, "regardless of the alleged crime of the victim, lynching in the twentieth century continued to be an important if illegal part of the system of punishment in the United States" (282).[6]

Franklin's work adds clarity to the subject of lynching by placing it in a historical context of the Black presence in America. Similarly, Trudier Harris' work, *Exorcising Blackness*, attests to the fact that the lynching portrayed in Brooks' poems represents the reality that lynching is a long acknowledged threat to Black life in America as well as an indicator of the "unempowered status" of Black people, both by its inclusion in historical references and its thematic treatment in myriad literary works (ix).[7] The fact that lynching is depicted in such a broad cross section of Black literature crossing both gender and genre is a statement on the need of Black writers to address historical circumstances which highlight the continued oppression in their cultural community. Although the subject of lynching functions as an "aside," or as integral to the thematic structure of a literature work, the fact that so many writers opted to include an incident points to the historical relevance and pain emanating from the act. Brooks, however, has a very specific reason for centering her poem "A Bronzeville Mother" around a lynching. She, like many notable black writers, "felt compelled to address the subject of lynching as a sign of the continued oppression of Blacks in America" (Harris 184).

Thus, fictionally as well as poetically, the theme of lynching has carved out a permanent niche in the realm of literature.

Brooks' treatment of several poems, however, veers away from these models in both her use of the ballad form and in the extensive psychological examination given to the perpetrators of the event as well as to the central characters. In "A Bronzeville Mother," Brooks handles the dual task of providing a succinct commentary on the horrors of racism in America while simultaneously addressing the sexism inherent in white male patriarchy and white female silence. Thematically, the central event of the poem is the 1955 lynching of a fourteen-year-old Chicago youth, Emmett Till, whose summer sojourn in Money, Mississippi, ended abruptly with his lynching after he allegedly made improper advances and "wolf-whistled" at a twenty-one-year-old white woman, Carolyn Bryant. Formulaically, Brooks exploits the structure of the traditional folk ballad and instead employs extensive artistic freedom in creating a literary ballad to encompass the tale.

Like the expertise exhibited by her predecessors, Sterling Brown's distinctive and prolific use of folk and literary ballads in *Southern Road* (1932) and Margaret Walker's ballad variations in *For My People* (1942), evidences of Brooks' technical proficiency in the traditional folk ballad form, as well as variations on its theme, are sprinkled throughout her canon. Noting that "the Afro-American ballad is like the ballad *qua sua,*" Gladys Williams engages in an examination of Brooks' extensive experimentation with the ballad form in "The Ballads of Gwendolyn Brooks" (206). She especially calls attention to the fact that while Brooks' poem "A Bronzeville Mother" "appears to unfold playfully in the form of the classical ballad," the ballad form is really the "muscular substructure," of the poem, rather than "something overlaying the material" (217).

In his study of *Native American Balladry*, G. Malcolm Laws specifically targets "the Negro's unusual powers of improvisation" in the creation of both folksongs and ballads.[8] Historically, Black poets have not only "recounted" a central event, but have gone further to embellish, enlarge, and otherwise decorate the tale for retelling. Likewise, in "A Bronzeville Mother," Brooks capitalizes upon the romanticism and chivalric quality inherent in the folk-ballad narrative, yet wields her own literary prowess to create a powerful rendition of a true-to-life event.

Factually, although the Till lynching had captured the attention of the media in glaring headlines across the nation, like *Jet* magazine's "Nation Horrified by Murder of Kidnaped Chicago Youth" and *Look* magazine's "The Shocking Story of Approved Killing in Mississippi" by William Bradford Huie, these accounts consistently focused upon the murdered Black youth and the two white males accused, tried, and acquitted of the lynching. Even in Stephen Whitfield's historical examination of the event in his book, *A Death in the Delta: The Story of Emmett Till,* scant attention was given to Carolyn Bryant, the white female in whose honor the deed was done. Thus, Brooks' artistic interpretation, besides providing a poetic commentary on America's social conditions, is a stellar achievement in its approach to female silence, since it recants the event from the point of view of an otherwise silenced white female. Interestingly enough, Bryant, who did not tell her husband of the event and apparently did not encourage retaliation against the youth for his alleged advances, was overridden and discounted by her husband who "felt compelled to react" after hearing of the incident from others (Whitfield 19). Much of her courtroom testimony was ruled inadmissible by the judge because of the lapse in time since the incident, and media accounts paid little heed to her views about the event as is evident by the omission of her account in most publications.

Look magazine, and others, however, did objectify her by featuring her picture regularly and taking note of her physical attributes, stating that she "is 21, five feet tall, weighs 103 pounds . . . an Irish girl with black hair and black eyes" (Huie

46) and that "she had won two beauty contests while in high school" (Whitfield 16). But other than attention to her physicality, Bryant became and remained a nonentity to those outside of her immediate community following the incident. Thus, Brooks' psychological profile ensconced in a motif of silence is a unique assessment of the mental meandering Bryant might actually have endured. That supposition remains intact because, unlike Huie's published interview of the white male perspectives on the incident, no similar interview of Bryant's rendition exists.[9]

Brooks opens the poem with the casually deliberate tone of mockery which insinuates the ludicrousness of the tale being depicted as a ballad since the third-person omniscient narrator is not cognizant of what really constitutes a ballad. Although to her mind, the event "had been like a / Ballad," in reality, "she had never quite / Understood" ballads (333). This initial distortion informs the later dismantling of the romanticism implied by the use of the ballad and thus calls into question the legitimacy of the entire social code of the South which condones the type of chivalry which permits murder. Although Brooks employs the abrupt entry to the poem, indicative of the ballad form, she quickly dispels any notion of adherence to a set formula. The traditional quatrain stanzaic pattern of the ballad is immediately replaced by an opening five-line stanza, followed by varying verse patterns throughout the poem. The formulaic *abcb* rhyme scheme of the traditional ballad is discarded for no rhyme, and the alternating tetrameter / trimeter metrical pattern is exchanged for irregular metrics. The artistic freedom Brooks exerts in the use of unrestricted metrics and inhibited stanzaic patterns enlarges the telescope through which a dual set of conditions, born in the aftermath of the lynching, can be examined. First, Brooks frees herself from the structures of prosodic formulas and creates a near prose narrative to explore the psychological complexities of Bryant's silence. She then probes the internal turmoil wrought upon the accused killer who, by virtue of a dubious court system which claimed that the uncovered body could not be definitively proven to be that of Till, was acquitted (Williams 45).

In the poem's second stanza, the extent to which the speaker needs to reorder her reality to a more palatable fantasy becomes clear. Using the stock images associated with the folk ballad, the heroine recreates "Herself: the milk-white maid, the 'maid mild' / Of the ballad. Pursued / by the Dark Villain. Rescued by the Fine Prince" (333). This level of romanticism permits the confused heroine to accept everything that has happened in anticipation of a "Happiness-Ever-After" life, once these unhappy events are put behind her. Yet these same romantic thoughts, culminating in the last line, "That made the breath go fast," are sharply redefined near the conclusion of the poem when she admits, "She heard no hoof-beat of the horse and saw no flash of / the shining steel" (328).

The steps she takes to get to the clarity that something has gone awry begin with her musings while she nervously prepares breakfast for her husband, "the Fine Prince," and burns the bacon. Because of what she does understand of the ballad, she suffers from the nagging thoughts that the "hacking down of a villain was more fun to think about / When his menace possessed undisputed breadth, undisputed / height, /And a harsh kind of vice" (334). And, since she has no knowledge of any evil deeds done by this "child," she is unable to accept his murder as right and justified. Her distraught mind is "disturbed" over the destruction of "a blackish child / Of fourteen, with eyes still too young to be dirty, / And a mouth too young to have lost every reminder / Of its infant softness" (334). Yet as the wife of the Fine Prince, she must accept this event as a part of the social code of the South which demands that as "Miss Southern White Woman," her reputation be unsullied, honor be avenged, purity remain intact, and that any criminal trespasser to these rules be duly punished, by death if necessary. If she is to continue to exist within the definitions of its stereotypes, created for the protectiveness of her femaleness, she must acknowledge and tolerate its racial stereotypes. Her limited focus on the situation is a direct result of the protected status of white women whose intellectual confinement made them victims to the very gender and racial stereotypes which held them captive. The narrator's reenactment of her psychological dilemma is indicative of the mental juggling which would be necessary to empower the Southern white women, who are controlled by a white patriarchal order designed to keep them away from Black men, not only to define themselves, but to redefine the people around them according to human, not merely racial, standards.

The real fear of Southern white men, that racial interaction and social equality of the races would lead to miscegenation and intermarriage between Black men and white women, has been the focus of several studies of race relations in America. Most pivotal is Myrdal's study of the antiamalgamation doctrine which culminates in a six-point schema, the "Rank Order of Discriminations," designed to convey the views of Blacks and whites on racial discrimination. When Myrdal asked Southern whites what they thought Black people wanted most, whites responded:

1. Sexual intercourse and intermarriage with white women
2. Social equality
3. Desegregation of public facilities including schools, churches, and means of transportation
4. Voting power
5. Equal justice
6. Economic empowerment (60)

The reality of these white suppositions is that when polled separately, Blacks provided the same assessment with a startling reversal. Myrdal writes: "*the Negro's own rank order is just about parallel, but inverse, to that of the white man.* The Negro resists least the discrimination on the ranks placed highest in the white man's evaluation and resents most any discrimination on the lowest level" (Myrdal's emphasis 61).

In *Sex and Racism in America,* Calvin Hernton adapts Myrdal's stance as a jumping off point for his ensuing discussion of race relations in America to reach his stark thesis that "the race problem is inexplicitly connected with sex" (4). As such, both Myrdal and Hernton provide the historical backdrop to understand that whatever advances "the black villain" might have made to "Miss White Southern Woman," white America was prepared to go beyond the pale of the law to send a death message to other Black males who might contemplate similar actions. The result, as Hernton writes, was that "sacred white womanhood emerged in the South as an immaculate mythology to glorify an otherwise indecent society" (16).[10]

Whether or not Emmett Till was "innocent" in his encounter and just playing out a boastful prank is the subject of controversy in several critical works. In *Against Our Wills*, Susan Brownmiller discusses cases where "black men had been put to death for coming too close to white women" and takes a hard line view of Till's actions (210). Although she condemns the lynching as "sheer outrageousness, for indefensible overkill with community support" (245), she also decries Till's alleged advances and argues that they "should not be misconstrued as an innocent flirtation," or a "kid's brash prank," but as "a deliberate insult just short of physical assault, a last reminder to Carolyn Bryant that this black boy, Till, had in mind to possess her" (247). Although Brownmiller opts to view Till's "theoretical intent" as a desire for sexual possession of Bryant, she, like the male writers mentioned, gives no credence to Bryant's perspective, but instead, uses her own voice to speak for Bryant in an attempt to determine Till's intentions, and ultimately contributes to the silence of omission which encloses Bryant. By reprimanding Till's actions so severely that they are rapidly escalated to the prominence of a national and pervasive sexism specifically among Black males, Brownmiller willfully ignores the historical proclivity for Southern white males to engage in random rapes and lynchings and the inherent racism and sexism initiated and controlled at their hands, as a trade-off for adding to the myth of the Black would-be-rapist as a worst-case-scenario. In doing so she misses her feminist calling of giving voice to Bryant's perspective on the incident, and like white males, opts instead to speak for Bryant by speaking for all women. Alice Walker counters the near hysteria in Brownmiller's interpretation by commenting that "Emmett Till was not a rapist. He was not even a man. He was a child who did not understand that whistling at a white woman could cost him his life" (66).

Brooks' poem does not detail the historic postures which created the right racial climate for the event to occur and to stimulate the critical sparring which later erupted over the specific nature of events or the intent of the murdered Till. Rather, she opts to move rapidly from the incident itself to the psychological ramifications on the woman by relating the stirring and dramatic tale with a controlled objectivity, as well as understating the horror of the events, except through the view of the woman. Though George Kent in *Blackness and the Adventure of Western Culture* sees problems which "to some degree entrap parts of most Southern located poems," because "the vibrations of history and culture push hard . . . making one wish to understand particulars," Brooks appropriately maintains the traditional impersonal distance inherent in the ballad, and relies on the well-known history of lynching in America generally, and the story of Emmett Till in particular (120).[11] The racist history of the South informs this and other poems succinctly, while the title and allusion to "magnolias" place the poem firmly in a Northern/Southern construction of racial tensions.

As a matter of fact, the fascinating thing about Brooks'

clever rendition of the central event in this poem, with no overt references to that event, is summed up in an assessment by Ezekiel Mphahlele in his *Voices in the Whirlwind*. He states:

> Miss Brooks is essentially a dramatic poet, who is interested in setting and character and movement. So that she is interested in those features of her people's life that go to define the setting of conflict, without any direct reference to the conflict itself. She is interested in bringing out in its subtlest nuances the color of life that conflict eventually creates. Her verse teems with words and phrases that represent motion and outward appearance, which in turn lead us to something deeper. (26)

The omniscient narrator, having dispensed with the technicalities of the ballad form, deftly begins to dismantle the persona of the "Fine Prince" as a paladin employed in the service of his palladium, the paragon of Southern virtue. Under a ruse of normalcy, adapted to hide the fact that "her composition / Had disintegrated," the woman clutches the last vestiges of her composure while she serves breakfast to her husband and children (319). But "The breaks were everywhere," and the husband's emotional stability is also at the point of rupture. He is accosted by memories of the crime as a media event; the meddlesome interlopers from the North whose intrusion added "unwanted fame" and notoriety to his otherwise normal life (336). His clear agitation points to America's history of Northern intolerance for Southern Jim Crow practices and the immediate stain to Mississippi's reputation because of Northern news coverage and political intervention in the case. The husband is disturbed:

> More papers were in from the North, he mumbled. More
> meddling headlines.
> With their pepper-words, "bestiality," and "barbarism,"
> and

> "Shocking."
> The half sneers he had mastered for the trial worked
> across
> His sweet and pretty face. (336)

He emerges as the face of the South deeply committed to its social codes and exhibits little tolerance for those Northern "intruders," especially symbolized by "that snappy-eyed mother. / That sassy, Northern, brown-black—," as well as the Northern media and politicians. His hostile posture further points to the South's bruised ego at the unwanted surveillance by her Northern brethren.

Under the pressure of these torturous memories, "the Fine Prince" ironically unveils his true colors and reveals himself as the "villain" who acts out his violent nature on his own children. The child's offense, tossing the "molasses [pitcher] in his brother's face," is too much for the Fine Prince to bear. He "leaned across the table and slapped / The small and smiling criminal," whereupon his hand now becomes "the Hand" which sends fear coursing through his wife's veins and snaps her into the reality of the authentically corrupt nature of the "Fine Prince." Brooks' fine use of synechdoche captures the internal agony of the husband who has been acquitted of murder, but who cannot shake his own self-incriminations.

Symbolically the red of the "bleeding headlines," representing the violence of the South, now covers their own lives. It is the "blood" she imagines on her child's face, "a lengthening red, a red that had no end" (338). When her husband touches her she imagines "a red ooze was seeping, spreading darkly, thickly, / slowly, / Over her white shoulders, her own shoulders, / And over all of Earth and Mars." And finally when he becomes amorous and kisses her, "His mouth, wet and red, / So very, very, very red," snaps her out of the romanticism implied in the ballad strains of the poem's opening lines. Yet even in the face of abuse to her children, she is unwittingly imprisoned by the social norms of her community, and consequently, the thoughts racing tumultuously through her head never gain voice. Her silence reigns supreme, for "She said not a word" in the face of "The fear, / Tying her as with iron" (338–9).

Suddenly flooding her psyche are all of the horrible memories which attest to the reality of a way of life that condones communal sentencing and punishment, based on racial parameters, for the presumption of wrongful deeds. She relives the circus atmosphere of the courtroom where the selling of Coca-Cola is raised to the level of importance of trial procedures, and visualizes the apparent shock and grief recreated as "Decapitated exclamation points in that Other Woman's / eyes" (339). The images flood over her insistently like a tidal wave threatening to drown her. Because she is groping for the clarity of vision which will lead to a full-blown sense of self-definition, autonomy, and humanity, she wrestles with the inner turmoil created by the social codes controlling her destiny. Finally, the hypnotic trance produced by the "perfume" of Mississippi's symbolic state flower, the magnolia, snaps her into the reality of "a hatred for him" as she at last realizes the magnitude of the crime and her role in it. In the final tercet:

> The last bleak news of the ballad.
> The rest of the rugged music.
> The last quatrain. (339)

She rejects the final romantic notions of the ballad and with it the Southern myth which has held her captive and rendered her mute.

In *A Life of Gwendolyn Brooks,* George Kent expresses concern that Brooks has attempted to enter the "the consciousness of a white character" and calls her portrayal of a Southern white woman "psychologically false" (142). He compares her attempt to the "disastrous consequences" of William Styron's portrayal of Nat Turner and notes the limited attempts of

William Faulkner to enter the consciousness of Black characters. Kent's negation of Brooks' character profile hinges on the compressed temporal movement of the poem, the lynching, acquittal, and the final cultural epiphany, which is a stylistic device associated with the ballad form. But once Bryant's awakening occurs, it becomes clear that the motif of women's silence, nurtured by a patriarchal society, would support the contention that although white women might have differed in their levels of racial awareness, they were not free to voice that difference for fear of being ostracized by their husbands and communities. As Kent stated earlier in *Blackness*, for him, Brooks' character "seems to arrive at the universal a bit too soon" (121). In an expanded view he writes:

> Where cultural and historical circumstances press a counter image upon the mind, the artist has more to do to show strain and struggle before the simple universal woman's heart emerges. It is a matter of charging artistic illusion with sufficient power. (*Life* 142)

By focusing on the "abrupt" burgeoning of Bryant's consciousness, Kent's interpretation invites consideration of the intense complexity of the historical relationship of Southern whites to their social code and suggests that no quick-fix solution could alter their racial perspectives. Yet, by engaging a motif of women's silence, Brooks has aptly depicted the psychological machinations of a woman entrapped in a patriarchal society she did not help to create. The woman has become empowered by awakening to the humanistic reality that her husband has murdered and been acquitted by a jury of his peers, yet rather than helping him, the act has unleashed the fury of his truly violent character which now may be rent upon his closest charges at any time: her and their children.

The portrait Brooks paints of the woman's awakening to an independent reality is a plausible one. What Brooks does not and cannot say is that one empowered white woman can alter the face of an entire Southern patriarchal society by virtue of her newly emerged clarity of vision. Yet the hope implicit in this awakening is that if one woman can awaken from such a terrible nightmare of existence, others may do the same, and ultimately if a groundswell of women give voice to their own sense of justice, they can eventually effect a difference in their individual destinies and ultimately in the collective destiny of America. Thus, Kent misses the mark entirely, by not understanding the ability of a woman to extricate herself psychologically from a system created extraneous to any consideration of her female psyche, but ironically, one that holds her a sexual and psychological hostage to empower the white male.

In a continuing examination of women, from the perspective of silence, the power of the companion piece to "A Bronzeville Mother," "The Last Quatrain of the Ballad of Emmett Till," lies in the definitive title, the apparent resistance to form, and in the contrasting imagery visible throughout the poem. The title neutralizes the evil inherent in the portrait of Till as a "Dark Villain" and restores his humanity by naming him. Though the title is suggestive of the ballad form, Brooks deliberately deviates from the true four-line stanza to an eight-line reordered quatrain:

> Emmett's mother is a pretty-faced thing;
>   the tint of pulled taffy.
> She sits in a red room,
>   drinking black coffee.
> She kisses her killed boy.
>   And she is sorry.
> Chaos in windy grays
>   through a red prairie. (340)

As such, by veering from the visual constraints of the ballad form, the poem offers an ironic commentary on the parallel deviation from strict judicial procedures in the Till murder investigation, trial, and acquittal.[12] Paradoxically, though the poem outwardly thwarts the ballad form, inwardly it adheres to the simplicity, abruptness, and stark imagery common to the ballad.

Brooks employs subtlety in the creation of contrasting images that connect "A Bronzeville Mother" and "The Last Quatrain." The Bronzeville mother who was viewed as "loiter[ing]" in Mississippi now "sits" in Chicago. In a static portrait, Till's mother conceals her pain and anguish in an aura of dignity as strong as the "black coffee" she drinks. By contrast, the psychological portrayal of the Mississippi mother reflects a woman whose mental state borders on inner turmoil and near hysteria.[13]

In the continuing use of contrasts, color symbolically permeates the tale as "red ooze" of violence in Mississippi now stains the landscape of Chicago in "a red room" and "a red prairie." Additionally, there is the contrast of loss as the sorrow apparent in the Bronzeville mother who "kisses her killed boy," stands in sharp contrast to the "hatred" of the Mississippi mother who can no longer bear her husband's kisses. Finally, as the poem closes, the line, "Chaos in windy grays" transports the theme of racial violence from its tragic origins in the Mississippi lynching to its emergence in the devastating public viewing and funeral services in Chicago. *Jet* magazine's searing headlines were in no way preparatory for the gruesome sight of the bloated and disfigured youth. Crowds of curious, sympathetic, and angry onlookers formed continuous lines for three days to confirm, visually, the horrors young Till had endured at the hands of his torturers (6).

Thematically, evidence of America's racial turbulence is also the subject of Brooks' "The Chicago *Defender* Sends a Man to Little Rock." Brooks draws upon the historic agenda of the Chicago *Defender* newspaper, founded in 1905, to report the ongoing instances of Southern racial violence which were of special concern to the Chicago community of Black Southerners, who, by virtue of the Great Migration, had been transplanted to Chicago, but, through the connection of family roots, still had vested interests in Southern occurrences. The poem's epigraph, "Fall, 1957," attests to the time frame of the violent repercussions to the nine Black students in Little Rock, Arkansas, who attempted to integrate the town's Central High School (346). Ostensibly, the first person narrator is befuddled by a community of whites who, seemingly normal in all other respects, nevertheless, stubbornly refused, in 1957, to permit nine Black students to attend school "with about two thousand white youngsters" (Williams 92), for fear of racial reprisals to the white students (97). Instead, white school board members and state legislators employed a variety of schemes, such as the "delayed implementation" of the Supreme Court decision, the creation of a "gradual approach" tactic to integration, and finally, the adoption of a state amendment to "circumvent" the order of the high court (93).

In a series of irregular stanza patterns, the first-person narrator reports on the many areas of normalcy he has witnessed in this Southern community of whites that is undergoing intense scrutiny by its concerned Northern brethren. Ultimately, this veneer of normalcy, apparent in Sunday churchgoing, placid Sunday afternoons filled with the social rituals of "lemon tea and Lorna Doones," community sponsored "baseball," and "Open Air Concert[s]," becomes a "puzzle" to the inquiring reporter as he juxtaposes these homey scenes with the racial reality of these same people "hurling spittle, rock," the "scythe / Of men harassing brownish girls," and bearing responsibility for the "bleeding brownish boy" he sees (346–48).

The sense of bewilderment expressed by the befuddled reporter is given voice when a portrait of common-everyday-folk is transmitted to the Northern newspaper office with the missive, "They are like people everywhere." The responsive couplet offers a single word query:

The angry Editor would reply
In hundred harryings of Why. (348)

Indeed, if the white people of Little Rock, Arkansas, are such a racially tolerant and cohesive community, as the poem suggests, what then could account for their noncompliance to the mandates of the 1954 *Brown* v. *the Board of Topeka, Kansas*, which called for the racial integration of Southern schools, especially since the school board of Little Rock was "the first in the South to issue a statement of compliance after the Supreme Court's ruling" (Williams 92). As Williams notes in *Eyes on the Prize*:

> From the mid-forties to the mid-fifties, blacks in Little Rock made dramatic gains. Some blacks had been allowed to join the police force, and in a few neighborhoods blacks and whites lived next door to one another. In contrast to their counterparts in most southern states, thirty-three percent of all eligible Arkansas blacks were registered to vote. The library, parks, and public buses had all been integrated, and in 1955 white schools seemed ready to open their doors to blacks. (92)

Thematically, Brooks poetically recants the atmosphere of Little Rock in 1957 as Blacks and whites struggled in a real life racial tug-of-war, further propelled by the intensity of political turmoil. The infamous Arkansas Governor Orval Faubus, whose own political aspirations were dependent upon keeping a contingency of powerful white segregationists placated so that he could continue his political climb, invested in school segregation as a means of gaining the necessary political clout to further his career (Williams 100). The implied violence, emanating in racial insults, and the real violence, perpetrated by physical acts inflicted upon the students, journalists, and photographers by "disorderly mobs" of angry citizens, continued until a "reluctant" President Eisenhower, hesitant to interfere with states rights, finally intervened by dispatching federal troops to Arkansas to protect the Little Rock Nine (101–107). Ultimately, Governor Faubus' strategies to avoid desegregation culminated in the 1958 closing of Little Rock's high schools for the entire school year. Paradoxically, that same year, "he won nomination for a third term as governor with an unprecedented sixty-nine percent of the vote," and in a 1958 Gallup Poll, was selected by Americans as "one of their ten most admired men."

This scenario of racial intolerance is the unspoken heart of Brooks' poem. The apparent details of the poem, offered as brief vignettes of everyday life in Little Rock, actually camouflage the real rage of a white community bent on resisting full racial integration at any cost.

> In Little Rock the people bear
> Babes, and comb and part their hair
> And watch the want ads, put repair
> To roof and latch. While wheat toast burns
> A woman waters multiferns. (*The Bean Eaters* 346)

The distinctive five-line opening stanza mirrors the complexity of the Little Rock situation in that poetically it lacks a cohesiveness because of its tercet and couplet variation. And while its rhythmic tetrameter metrical pattern supports the idea of pastoral verse and easy, unsophisticated melodies, the erratic stanzaic pattern throughout eventually signifies a situation which hides its racial horrors beneath a poetic veneer. Thus, Brooks' technical use of varied verse forms and metrics is informed by the complexity of the dual faces of humanity in Little Rock.

Likewise, the consistency of rhyme, both full and slant, supports the idea of a community content with outward compliance to social rituals, while internally still struggling to come to full realization of social equality. And though Brooks opens with an ambiguous reference to "the people" of Little Rock, which might be inclusive of all its residents, Black and white, the later reference to the "they" who are "hurling spittle, rock," identifies the angry mobs of whites who daily met and taunted the Little Rock Nine (Williams 107).

The first of the two final single-line stanzas of the poem, "The lariat lynch-wish I deplored" (*The Bean Eaters* 348), is suggestive of the real life threats consistently verbalized against the Little Rock Nine as they daily entered Central High School under federal guards on duty to protect them from hostile bystanders who often called for their "lynching" (Williams 102). The final line, "The loveliest lynchee was our Lord," recaptures the earlier hints of the religious rituals of a people who "sing / Sunday hymns," adhere to "testament and tunes," and who "love," yet who, by contrast, are still grappling with the notion of social equality (*The Bean Eaters* 348). Thus, they continue to taunt, insult, and inflict violence upon the racially different school children in hopes of forestalling full integration. In conjunction, the two stanzas are mindful of the lynching of Christ, yet in an ironic antithesis of interpretation, also function as an unfortunate statement on the historic potential for the tenets of Christianity to sit comfortably along side the cruelty of lynching.

This final line of Brooks' poetic social commentary on Southern racial tensions captures the meshing of race and religion in Countee Cullen's sonnet "Christ Recrucified," which opens, "The South is crucifying Christ again." Thus, Cullen's poem also addresses the theme of the people of the South who are "like people everywhere," yet many of whom have a predilection, reminiscent of Christ's crucifixion, for violence against Black people. Similarly, Brooks establishes a thematic parallel between the crucified Christ and the mistreated Southern Black man by ending the poem on a note often visible in the works of Cullen.[14]

The final poem in *The Bean Eaters* which explicitly

expounds upon the theme of violence perpetrated against Blacks in America is "The Ballad of Rudolph Reed." Briefly, the poem sings the tale of a poor, urban, Black man who, in an attempt to grasp the fringes of the American Dream, integrates an all-white residential area and encounters the wrath of his new white neighbors who are irate at his intrusion. Slowly, yet with the insistent rage of a distant storm gaining a thunderous momentum, Reed responds to their acts of violence with recognition, resistance, and finally, retaliation. Historically, the poem has its antecedents in the real life situation which occurred on Chicago's far South Side in the early 1950s and was captured in Frank London Brown's novel, *Trumbull Park* (1959), a fictionalized version of the violent racial clashes between Blacks and whites, and Dempsey Travis' *The Autobiography of Black Chicago* (1981) a journalistic report of the those events. In the 1950s, the Trumbull Park Housing Projects could offer the working class a clean, decent place to live at affordable prices and, with well over 400 family units, was sought after by both Black and white blue-collar workers. But when Black families began integrating, over 1,200 policemen were dispatched to the area for several months before the nightly eruptions of violence against the new Black residents ceased. As Travis states, "The siege of Trumbull Park was the longest and most costly racial incident in Chicago History" (132). By focusing her poetic lens on a single Black family, Brooks reconstructs memories of these devastating racial clashes, thereby enlarging the portrait of the violent racial encounters as a microcosm of America's dismal integration efforts in urban housing.

Brooks' choice of the ballad form to tell the fatal tale of Rudolph Reed encompasses both her epic tendency to swell a story to its most grandiose proportions, as evident in "The Anniad" (*Annie Allen*), as well as her stylistic penchant for the compression and economy of "The Last Quatrain of the Ballad of Emmett Till." In the first four stanzas of "The Ballad of Rudolph Reed," the poem basically adheres to the *abcb* rhyme scheme and the tetrameter or trimeter metrics, though longer line length intermittently expands meaning throughout the poem. The third-person narrator details Reed's poverty-stricken existence in the opening stanza:

> Rudolph Reed was oaken.
> His wife was oaken too.
> And his two good girls and his good little man
> Oakened as they grew. (376)

The first of dual implications of "oaken" initially delineates only the racial classification of Reed and his "dark" family, yet by stanza five a second concept is evident (376). The innate qualities of the oak tree—the strength, endurance, and perseverance in the face of adversity—characterize Reed, who announces that he will "fight" for his home when he finds it (377). And in stanza seven, the real estate agent, with a creeping awareness, reassesses Reed's strength:

> The agent's steep and steady stare
> Corroded to a grin.
> *Why, you black old, tough old hell of a man,*
> *Move your family in!* (Brooks' emphasis 377)

Coupled with the efficacy of dual meanings in the poem, the alliterative sensibilities attached to Rudolph Reed's name evoke the musical and rhythmic quality of the ballad, while again attesting to the pliability, yet resilience, of Reed. The symbolic representation of Rudolph Reed's strength is woven throughout the poem in a series of images that reflect the tensions emerging from his evolving sense of recognition of the impending battle. When Reed ventures into "a street of bitter white" to select a home for his family, his demeanor is in decided contrast to that of the caustic real estate agent:

> Nary a grin grinned Rudolph Reed,
> Nary a curse cursed he,
> But moved in his House. With his dark little wife,
> And his dark little children three. (377)

In his happy naiveté, Rudolph Reed is "too joyous to notice" the hostile glares of his neighbors, and even the nightly rain of rocks tossed through his window extract no immediate reaction. But finally, the violent stain of his daughter's blood disturbs his patience, "But he looked, and lo! small Mabel's blood," and the larger than life figure of Reed armed with a history of racism and pain, surges forth like an erupting volcano, ready to do battle with his "thirty-four," his "butcher knife," and the unleashed fury of his residual rage for being a disrespected, and thus, unempowered Black man in America. The hint of his self-contained rage resides in the repetition of "Nary a curse cursed he," as though as long as Reed restrained his words, he could restrain the need to retaliate against the taunting mob. But, eventually, just as "the words in his mouth were stinking," the emotional tightrope gripping Reed's composure snaps, and "He was no longer thinking" (378).

> By the time he had hurt his fourth white man
> Rudolph Reed was dead.
> His neighbors gathered and kicked his corpse.
> "Nigger—" his neighbors said. (378)

Brooks carries off "The Ballad of Rudolph Reed" with technical brilliance as the strains of the folk ballad strive to fathom the changing disposition of Reed. The insistent rhythm of the tetrameter and trimeter drives the ballad along forcefully like the malicious fervor of the ensuing mob and the rage of Reed. The use of stylistic devices like polyptoton, alliteration, and anaphora paints a portrait of a man prepared to forge ahead and die for his right to live the American Dream. The inevitable symbolism of the red of violence visible in "small Mabel's blood" is the final testament to a man bent on integrating an all-white residential area as a means of improving his family's housing needs, but who is destined by the racial history of the times to meet with violent opposition. In the poem's final stanza, the outcome of the brutal battle is clear:

> Small Mabel whimpered all night long,
> For calling herself the cause.
> Her oak-eyed mother did no thing
> But change the bloody gauze. (378)

The mother, a model of quiet determination as emphasized by her oaken eyes, stoically figures as future head-of-household as she "change[s] the bloody gauze" (378). During the course of the ballad, Reed moves from recognition, to resistance, and finally, to retaliation, by attempting to meet the force of the white mob on its own terms. Brooks makes superb use of the ballad form to sing of the courage, resolve, and yet ultimate tragedy of Rudolph Reed. While probing the electrically charged race relations that produce the dialectic of the American Dream, she ironically elevates Reed to a heroic place and, thus, makes extraordinary what has heretofore been deemed as less than ordinary.

The overriding theme in *The Bean Eaters* is the continuing commentary which defines America from the multiple perspectives of race, gender, and class. Gwendolyn Brooks' 1960 book of poetry, while perhaps not intentionally "social" in its topical persuasion, certainly has ample access to the most momentous events of the pre–Civil Rights Movement to serve as a back-drop to her continuing surveillance of the Chicago community of Bronzeville and capture the hearts, minds, and movements of the people as they react to these national occurrences.

Brooks is indeed "awake" during these years prior to her formal "awakening" at the 1967 Fisk Black Writers Conference in Nashville, Tennessee. She offers poetic utterances on the movements of her characters throughout the urban landscape, and the voice of social consciousness emerges as she assiduously reports on the middle-class dilemmas, gender issues, intraracial color struggles, economic deprivation, segregation and discrimination, social inequality, and violence which intrude upon the lives and livelihoods of her Bronzeville neighbors. Although the formulistic tenets of prosody are not so explicitly evident in *The Bean Eaters* as in *A Street in Bronzeville*, and most prominently in *Annie Allen*, Brooks' voice here, more clearly than in any previous work, emits the strains of rage, ensconced in language so beautifully rendered as to make the work palatable and enduring, yet social, as it versifies America's continuing tolerance of racial inequality. As poet, metrically, she uses her touch to confront, defy, exploit, and challenge the notion that everything in America is status quo. She alters stanzaic patterns, opting to lengthen, expand, and regularly alternate them as though in mockery of America's inconsistent adherence to the laws of democracy. Brooks' finesse with her craft is astute. There is no mistaking her expertise and one is always aware that if she employs inconsistent metrics, nonce stanzaic arrangements, off and slant, rather than full rhyme, and multiple schemes and tropes, these devices serve to illuminate situations, incidents, and events that, too, are off kilter. As such, her masterful strokes have not really changed from her earliest poetic efforts. Rather, she has accommodated the tenor of the times, the tumultuous fifties, and parallels that period poetically.

Coda for a Landscape Revisited

The early works of Gwendolyn Brooks, *A Street in Bronzeville* (1945), *Annie Allen* (1949), and *The Bean Eaters* (1960) are a poetic expression of social commentary on the racial, social, and economic climate of the 1940s and 1950s for Black Americans. Brooks fulfills the role of urban reporter as she gleans the landscape of Bronzeville and creates a poetic chronicle of both implicit and explicit commentaries on the Black impoverished community. Houston Baker notes her contribution in "The Achievement of Gwendolyn Brooks":

> [Brooks] has spoken forcefully against the indignities suffered by Black Americans in a racialistic society: she was one of the heralds of today's black revolutionary consciousness and is currently serving as one of its most important artistic guides. (*CLA* 31)

Since 1945 she has melded her artistic and social purpose to awaken her cultural community to the realities of their impoverished plight in the Black Metropolis of America, while simultaneously displaying the artistic craftsmanship that has secured her position in the annals of literary history.

A Street in Bronzeville is a metaphor for Black, urban, ghetto life in America. It is the artistic reins held taut by Brooks—her emotional control, clarifying distance, and ironic tone—that steer the work from a tragic victim analysis to a heroic portrait of ghetto survival and cultural identification. *Annie Allen* is the lyrical cry to the Black women of Bronzeville to grasp the power of womanhood that will strengthen them and redefine the future for their children. Brooks' structural complexity is especially evident in "The Anniad," where she parodies lofty classical stanzaic patterns to treat the subject of stymied ghetto lives as an implicit criticism of America's dual social order. And finally, in *The Bean Eaters*, Brooks reaches a heightened level of social commentary as she articulates the social climate that precipitated the Civil Rights Movement.

The period of 1945–1960 was one of confrontation with classical forms for Brooks. Her early canon supports the contention that her seeming compliance to conventional form, as in the sonnet and ballad, was really a subversive act of poetic redefinition to articulate her views on the social climate for Black Americans. Brooks persistently defied conventional forms, meter, and rhyme with myriad modifications, divergences, variances, and adaptations to mask her message of social commentary and render it more palatable for her early white audience.

Notes

Notes to A Critical Context

1. Paul M. Angle, *We Asked Gwendolyn Brooks.* (Chicago: Illinois Bell Telephone, Summer, 1967) rpt. in and hereafter cited from Gwendolyn Brooks, *Report From Part One* (Detroit: Broadside, 1972) 141. Among the tributes made to her in *Say That the River Turns: The Impact of Gwendolyn Brooks* (ed. Haki R. Madhubuti, Chicago: Third World P, 1987), Brooks' husband, Henry Blakely II, remarks that prior to their marriage, he had noticed her "shyness" (6). Brooks' daughter, Nora Brooks Blakely comments that "many people see Gwendolyn Brooks as a shy, retiring, quiet sort of person" (7). And Abena Joan Brown counts Brooks as one of "the quiet, strong stalwart ones" (16).

2. Brooks, *Report From Part One* (84).

3. J. Saunders Redding, "Cellini-Like Lyrics," *Saturday Evening Review* 17 Sept. 1949: 23, 27; "The Negro Writer—Shadow and Substance," *Phylon* XI (1950): 371–73; David Littlejohn, *Black on White: A Critical Survey on Writing by American Negroes* (New York: Grossman, 1966) 90; Babette Deutsch, *Yale Review* 39 (1950): 362. Each of these critics took specific and extensive interest in the craftsmanship of *Annie Allen.*

4. Margaret Walker, "New Poets," *Phylon* XI (1950): 355–60. Walker embarks upon a fine assessment of Brooks' "excellent knowledge of form" as an argument against the "obscurantist" charges "levelled at *Annie Allen.*" Contrary to Walker's perspective is that of Richard Barksdale in "Contemporary Poetry," *Phylon* XIX (1958): 408–16, who views Brooks as one of the new

younger poets who replicates the poetic masters, including T. S. Eliot and Ezra Pound. Although Barksdale names young poets such as Robert Hayden and Robert Lowell, he consistently manages to focus in on Brooks' *Annie Allen* as his primary example of the concentration on form, especially compression, to the exclusion of content and meaning.

5. Hortense J. Spillers, "Gwendolyn the Terrible: Propositions on Eleven Poems," *Shakespeare's Sisters: Feminist Essays on Women Poets*, eds. Sandra M. Gilbert and Susan Gubar (Bloomington: Indiana UP, 1979). Spillers makes an astute observation on Brooks' regional and urban focus: "With a taste for the city and an ear for change, Gwendolyn Brooks restores the tradition of citizen–poet" (244).

6. Keneth Kinnamon, "Call and Response: Intertextuality in Two Autobiographical Works by Richard Wright and Maya Angelou," *Studies in Black American Literature: Belief vs. Theory in Black American Literary Criticism*, ed. Joe Weixlmann and Chester J. Fontenot (Greenwood, Florida: Penkevill, 1986) 133.

7. St. Clair Drake and Horace Cayton, *Black Metropolis: A Study of Negro Life in a Northern City*. Vol. 1 (1945; New York: Harcourt, Brace, and World P, rpt. 1962; U of Chicago P, 1993) xvii–xxxiv. In the 1945 introduction, Richard Wright addresses the "rage and impotent despair" that results from the type of racial exclusion the American Negro faces. The subject of racial rejection is also a target of Drake and Cayton's discussion in *Black Metropolis* 390.

8. Gwendolyn Brooks, *Blacks* (Chicago: Third World P, 1987). A collection of Brooks' works, including: *A Street in Bronzeville* (1945); *Annie Allen* (1949); *Maud Martha* (1953); *The Bean Eaters* (1960); *In the Mecca*

(1968); and selections from *Primer for Blacks* (1991); *Beckonings* (1975); *To Disembark* (1981); and *The Near-Johannesburg Boy* (1971). All parenthetical references cited in the text are taken from *Blacks*.

Notes to Chapter One

1. This manuscript of thirty–three poems is in the Lilly Library at Indiana University, Bloomington, Indiana.

2. Michael Fabre, *The Unfinished Quest of Richard Wright*, trans. Isabel Barzun (New York: William Morrow, 1973). Fabre notes that Wright "began his literary career as a revolutionary poet" (95); Robert Felgar, *Richard Wright* (Boston: Twayne, 1980) 27–29, and Constance Webb, *Richard Wright: A Biography* (New York: Putman, 1968) 119–125 make references to the publication of Wright's poetry in journals like *New Masses, Anvil,* and *Left Front* between 1933 and 1934.

3. Robert Bone, "Richard Wright and the Chicago Renaissance," *Callaloo* 9.3–28 (1986): 446–468; Craig Werner, "Leon Forrest, the AACM and the Legacy of the Chicago Renaissance," *Black Scholar* 23.3–4 (1993): 10–14; these works define the Black presence in the Chicago Renaissance. Werner writes: "One of the most important revisions of 20th Century Afro-American cultural history focuses on the significance of Chicago between the mid–1930s and the mid–fifties" (11).

4. Allan H. Spear, *Black Chicago: The Making of a Negro Ghetto 1890–1920* (Chicago: U of Chicago P, 1967). See Spear's discussion of "The Physical Ghetto" (11-27). In *Black Metropolis*, Drake and Cayton reveal the origin of the name "Bronzeville": after noting that "'Ghetto' is a harsh term, carrying overtones of poverty

and suffering, of exclusion and subordination," they write that the name Bronzeville seems to have been coined by "an editor of the Chicago *Bee*, who, in 1930, sponsored a contest to elect a 'Mayor of Bronzeville.' A year or two later, when this newspaperman joined the *Defender* staff, he took his brain–child with him" (383), which may explain Brooks' comment that the name "was invented by the Chicago *Defender* long, long ago to refer to the then black area (*RPO* 160)."

5. Michael Flug, "Vivian Gordon Harsh," *Black Women in America: An Historical Encyclopedia*, Vol. 1, ed. Darlene Clark Hine (Bloomington: Indiana UP, 1993) 542–3.

6. Harsh's Special Negro Collection was originally housed at the George Cleveland Hall Branch Library, on the corner of 48th Street and South Michigan Avenue in Chicago. It was revived after the Civil Rights Movement of the 1960s, and in 1970 it was renamed the Vivian G. Harsh Research Collection of Afro–American History and Literature. Currently it is located at the Carter G. Woodson Regional Library of Chicago, Illinois.

7. See Fabre (95); Felgar (27–25); Webb (119–125) on Wright's poetry.

8. Kitty Chapelle, "Colored Culture in Chicago," Illinois Works Project (9/14/37, unpublished papers held in the Harsh Collection) 3.

9. Bone, "Chicago Renaissance" argues compellingly that the Chicago Renaissance rivaled the Harlem Renaissance in terms of literary output (446–449).

10. George Kent, *A Life Of Gwendolyn Brooks* (Kentucky: U of Kentucky P, 1990), engages in a lengthy discussion of Brooks' early writing and publishing experiences, 7, 24, 26, 40, 64.

11. The demographics of Bronzeville are noted in sev-

eral sources: Drake and Cayton, *Metropolis* 384; Jontyle Theresa Robinson and Wendy Greenhouse, *The Art of Archibald J. Motley, Jr.* (Chicago: Chicago Historical Society, 1991) 40; "A Golden Spot for Literature," *Chicago Sun Times* 21 Feb. 1991:31.

12. Drake and Cayton, *Metropolis*, 13, 16. E. Franklin Frazier, *The Negro Family In Chicago* (Chicago: U of Chicago P, 1932) 92.

13. Robinson and Greenhouse, *Motley* 40. Drake and Cayton, *Metropolis* 13–18.

14. Gunnar Myrdal, *An American Dilemma: The Negro Problem and Modern Democracy* (New York: Harper & Brothers, 1944). Myrdal discusses "Housing Conditions" in Chapter 16, "Housing Segregation" and "Sanctions for Residential Segregation" in Chapter 26. Drake and Cayton, *Metropolis* 178. Frank London Brown, *Trumbull Park* (Chicago: Regency, 1959). Brown's novel is a fictionalized account of the real-life racial violence that was prompted by the integration of a Chicago Housing Project on the far south side of the city. Robinson and Greenhouse, *Motley* 41.

15. Drake and Cayton, *Metropolis* 383. The authors discuss the origin of Bronzeville, the "mock–elections" of officials, and annual parades that led to a sense of community in the Black Belt. And, the article, "Walter L. Lowe, insurance executive and the last Mayor of Bronzeville, dies," *Chicago Defender* 4 Aug. 1992: 3, confirms the longevity of the practice of selecting businessmen to represent the community within its enclave, as well as in the broad civic sector.

16. Information on the more well–known community institutions provided by Dempsey Travis, *Autobiography of Black Chicago* (Chicago: Urban Research Institute, 1981) 77; Drake and Cayton, *Metropolis* 380, 383; and

Robinson and Greenhouse, *Motley*, 47.

17. In *Metropolis*, Drake and Cayton introduce and define the five "Axes of Life" that represent the aspirations of Bronzevillians (385). Also, Robinson and Greenhouse, in *Motley*, do a fine job of cataloging Archibald Motley's artwork based upon his emphasis in the night life and religious ceremony in the Bronzeville community (46). They note that in the broad spectrum of his work, Motley was "indifferent" to the theme of work, and perhaps duly so, given the limited access to employment for Black people (44). But, as the authors appropriately note, as "an astute observer of the world around him, Motley eschewed grand social theories and political agendas; his goal was simply to record his world as completely and honestly as he could" (1).

18. Brooks, *RPO* 57.

Notes to Chapter Two

1. Gwendolyn Brooks, *A Street in Bronzeville* (1945), rpt. in *Blacks* (Chicago: Third World P, 1987) 17–75.

2. Richard Wright, "Introduction: Blueprint for Negro Writing," *New Challenge*, II (Fall 1937), rpt. in *The Black Aesthetic*, ed. Addison Gayle, Jr. (Garden City, New York: Doubleday/Anchor, 1971) 315–326. In a discussion of the "segregated channels" of Negro life in America, Wright notes: "There is a Negro church, a Negro press, a Negro social world, a Negro sporting world, a Negro business world, a Negro school system, Negro professions; in short, a Negro way of life in America. The Negro people did not ask for this, and deep down, though they express themselves through their institutions and adhere to this special way of life, they do not want it now. This special existence was forced upon them from without by lynch

rope, bayonet and mob rule. They accepted these negative conditions with the inevitability of a tree which must live or perish in whatever soil it finds itself" (319). Also see John Hope Franklin's discussion of "The Negro World," *From Slavery to Freedom* (New York: Knopf, 1988) 376–380.

3. Drake and Cayton's *Metropolis* is especially pertinent for a discussion of the origins of "The Axes of Life" and the study that produced them (385).

4. Similar to the poetic creations of Bronzeville by Brooks, and the view of social scientists Drake and Cayton, Archibald Motley, Jr.'s artistic portraitures of "having a good time" and "worshiping the Lord" in his "Bronzeville" series offer vivid portrayals of life in the community. His work is analyzed in Robinson and Greenhouse, *Motley*.

5. In *Dilemma*, Myrdal discusses the housing difficulties of Negroes in Chicago and points out: "the constant immigration of Southern Negroes into this segregated area caused doubling–up of families, the taking in of lodgers, the conversion of once spacious homes and apartments into tiny flats, the crowding of an entire family into a single room, the rapid raising of rents, the use of buildings which should be condemned" (1127).

6. D. H. Melhem, *Gwendolyn Brooks: Poetry and the Heroic Voice* (Lexington: U of Kentucky P, 1987) 22. The author's explication of the "interior view" of "kitchenette building" augments her view of "entrapment as the major theme of the work.

7. Melhem, *Heroic*. The author discusses the 1962 controversy stemming from the "political overtones" of the line "Nothing but a plain black boy" that caused both a New York and a Los Angeles radio station to ban both the poem and Oscar Brown Jr.'s 1962 musical version,

("Elegy for a Plain Black Boy," Columbia) 31, 132. See also George Kent, *A Life of Gwendolyn Brooks* (Lexington: U of Kentucky P, 1990) 154.

8. Hettie Jones, *Big Star Fallin' Mama: Five Women in Black Music* (New York: Dell, 1974). Also, Gary Smith, "*A Street in Bronzeville,* The Harlem Renaissance and the Mythologies of Black Women," *Contemporary Poets,* ed. Harold Bloom (New York: Chelsea, 1986) 43–56. Smith correctly differentiates between the blues star featured in Sterling Brown's poem "Ma Rainey" and Mame when he states: "But where Ma Rainey is realized as a mythic goddess within black folk culture, Mame is shown to be the double victim of sexual and racial exploitation" (52).

9. Several sources comment on the social stigma attached to abortion: Suzanne Juhasz, "Gwendolyn Brooks and Nikki Giovanni," *Naked and Fiery Forms: Modern American Poetry By Women* (New York: Octagon, 1976) notes the power of the poem as "a controversial social statement expressed with eloquence" whose "universality" of language is intended to "legitimize the particular mother—to make reputable the socially disreputable" (153). In "A Quilt in Shades of Black: The Black Aesthetic in Twentieth-Century American Poetry," Seibles notes that "one senses a private guilt. . . a solitary torment" (175). And Smith, in "Mythologies," sees an "alienated, seemingly disaffected narrator of 'the mother' who laments the loss of her children but with the resurgent, hopeful voice that closes the poem. . . "(46). Kent, *A Life* shares the view that of all the poems in *A Street in Bronzeville,* "the only poem [Richard Wright] did not like was 'the mother'. . . Wright did not feel that the poet had yet appeared who could lift abortion to the poetic plane'" (63). Kent also notes of Brooks' 1980 invitation to read poetry at the White House by for-

mer President Jimmy Carter and Mrs. Carter: "One of the selections that she read was 'the mother,' her still–controversial poem on abortion" (259).

10. Brooks in her first autobiography, *RPO*, comments: "A dark–complexioned girl just didn't have a chance if there was light–skinned competition. In grammar school I got my first introduction to the fact that bias could exist among our people, too" (172).

11. Langston Hughes, "Blue Bayou," *Jim Crow's Last Stand*, (Atlanta: Negro Publishing Society of America, 1943) 10, rpt. in *One Way Ticket*, (New York: Knopf, 1949) 53 and *Selected Poems of Langston Hughes* (New York: Knopf, 1959) 170. Hughes' poem, centered around a Southern white man and Black woman, offers an interesting reversal of the violence that is common to interracial relationships. Also see Sterling Brown's, "Frankie and Johnny," in Michael S. Harper, *The Collected Poems of Sterling A. Brown* (New York: Harper, 1980) 44.

12. A recent work that highlights the continuing conflicts of color prejudices in the Black community is Kathy Russell, Midge Wilson, and Ronald Hall's *The Color Complex: The Politics of Skin Color Among African Americans* (New York: Harcourt Brace, 1992). Brooks comments that the authors "have put together numerous aspects, responses, and illuminations invaluable to any study of this peculiar subject" (Back Cover).

13. Elise Johnson McDougald, "The Task of Negro Womanhood," *The New Negro: An Interpretation*, ed. Alain Locke (1925; New York: Arno, 1968) 369–382. As an example of the restrictions placed on employment opportunities for Black women, McDougald states: "In the great mercantile houses, the many young Negro girls who might be well suited to sales positions are barred

from all but menial positions. . . in spite of the claims of justice and proved efficiency, telephone and insurance companies and other corporations which receive considerable patronage from Negroes deny them proportionate employment" (373).

14. McDougald notes that the Negro woman "realizes that the ideals of beauty, built up in the fine arts, have excluded her almost entirely. Instead, the grotesque Aunt Jemimas of the streetcar advertisements proclaim only an ability to serve, without grace of loveliness" (370).

15. In *Fiery Forms*, Juhasz struggles with "the distance inherent in and essential to [Brooks'] approach" especially as it relates to a feminist perspective. She states: "Women have always been prominent as subject matter for her poems, but she has written about them as about everything else, as subject, never as self" (151).

16. W. E. B. Du Bois, *Souls of Black Folk* (1903; New York: Bantam, 1989) 3. Houston A. Baker, Jr. "The Achievement of Gwendolyn Brooks," *CLA* 1(1972), 23–31. In asserting a sense of double–consciousness in the works of both Du Bois and Brooks, Baker states: "The high style of both authors, . . . is often used to explicate the condition of the black American trapped behind a veil that separates him from the white world" (23). Of Brooks he notes: "Beset by a double–consciousness, she has kept herself from being torn asunder by speaking the truth in poems that equal the best work in the black and the white American literary traditions" (31).

17. R. Baxter Miller, "'Does Man Love Art?': The Humanistic Aesthetic of Gwendolyn Brooks," ed. *Black American Literature and Humanism* (Kentucky: U of Kentucky P, 1981) 95–112. Interestingly, Miller sees the

"introspective and questioning tone" Brooks adopts in "The Sundays of Satin–Legs Smith" as a product of her early prointegrationist stance and consequent "concern for a White audience," but argues that in her later poetry her "voice became more definite" (98).

18. Du Bois, *Souls* (3). Satin–Legs' blindness also recalls the use of the blindness motif in Ralph Ellison's *The Invisible Man* (New York: Signet, 1952). C.W.E. Bigsby, "The Black Poet as Cultural Sign," *The Second Black Renaissance: Essays in Black Literature* (Westport, Conn: Greenwood P, 1980) 257–301. Bigsby defines Satin as "unconcerned at the restrictive boundaries defined by remote and largely unfelt forces" (273). Harry B. Shaw, "Perceptions of Men by Gwendolyn Brooks," *Black American Poets Between Worlds, 1940–1960*, ed. R. Baxter Miller (Knoxville: U of Tennessee P, 1986) 136–159. In a discussion of Satin–Legs' "impotence," Shaw sees him as "Having to live the life of illusion while shunning his own identity, he is a subtle victim of the larger society that denies him free access to the American Dream" (142).

19. Melhem, *Heroic*, calls Satin–Legs' "clear delirium" "Brooks' oxymoron for an ecstatic residue" (33), while Miller views it as "Satin's confusion. . . yet the phrase clarifies a double consciousness working in the poem where the narrator's thinking occasionally merges with that of Satin–legs'" (97).

20. Kent, *A Life*, identifies a white observer and states: "The drama of the poem arises from the presence of a speaker and a white observer of conventional notions who is being indicted as a representative of the depriving society" (68).

21. Du Bois, *Souls*, asserts that "the healing of this vast sore" of "social separation and acute race–sentive-

ness," calls for "social surgery." Yet, he acknowledges that "the very voices that cry hail to this good work are, strange to relate, largely silent or antagonistic to the higher education of the Negro" (73), and further argues: "Here, then, is the plain thirst for training; by refusing to give this Talented Tenth the key to knowledge, can any sane man imagine that they will lightly lay aside their yearning and contentedly become hewers of wood and drawers of water?" (74).

22. Although in *Fiery Forms*, Juhasz argues that "Brooks at no time speaks in a personal or a private voice . . . does not participate in the drama . . . [and] does not speak in the lyric voice . . . the voice of the self," the absence of first–person phrasing should not be misconstrued to mean that Brooks' lyrical message goes unheeded (151). Robert H. Glauber, rev. of *Selected Poems*, "Our Miss Brooks: Lyricist," *Chicago Sun-Times* 22 Sept. 1963: 1–2. In a discussion of Brooks' poetry since her 1945 volume, Glauber applauds the fact that Brooks' "biting and provocative social criticism" does not diminish the "lyric vision" of her poetry and cites Satin–Legs as one of her "memorable characters" (2). Brooks' lyrical tone in the quoted lines identifies the emotional involvement of the narrator and foreshadows the lyrical tones of the closing stanza. And, on a different note, Eugene B. Redmond, *Drumvoices: A Critical History*, offers a historical focus on Satin–Legs' attire when he writes: [Satin–Legs] goes to a wardrobe that, when inventoried, sounds like a replay of the whole era of the zootsuiter and the bebopper" (275). Brooks, *RPO*, likens him to the "zootsuiters" of the 1940s and writes: They were not only black men but Puerto Ricans, too, who would wear these suits with the wide shoulders, and the pants did balloon out and then come down to

tapering ends, and they wore chains . . ." (155).

23. Du Bois, *Souls* (23). Franklin, *Slavery*, comments that the results of urban problems revealed that "the vast majority of Negro youth did not get an opportunity to share in the American dream of equal opportunities. They pointed out that the environment of Negro youth often forced them to react in a manner that many regard as shiftless, irresponsible, and aggressive" (382).

24. The idiomatic phrase, "The alarm clock meddling in somebody's sleep" recalls the young woman in "obituary for a living lady" who "Worried the windows" and in Henderson, *Poetry*, the poetic use of the folk expression "Worrying the line" (41).

25. Myrdal, *Dilemma*, is informative about the issue of vagrancy and loitering as it emerged at the end of the Civil War for the unemployed freedmen (n7 1234).

26. Henderson, *Poetry*, comments on how Brooks "assumes knowledge of the popular Black songs, but in order to create the proper contrast, she delineates the essential quality of the European composers whom she mentions" (48).

27. Conceived from the live blues performances at some of Chicago's famous night spots such as the Cabaret de Champion, the Savoy Ballroom, and the Dreamland, Motley's paintings, "Blues" (1929) and "Saturday Night" (1935) offer a lively depiction of colorful cabaret life of Chicago's blues–loving community, during the heyday of blues entertainment (Robinson 47–48).

28. Ralph Ellison, "Richard Wright's Blues," *Shadow and Act* (New York: Signet, 1966) 89–105, rpt. in *Black Writers of America*, eds. Richard Barksdale and Keneth Kinnamon (New York: Macmillan, 1972) 686–693. Ellison uses the phrase when he references the "almost

surreal image of a black boy singing lustily as he probes his own grievous wound" (686).

29. Calvin C. Hernton, *Sex and Racism in America* (New York: Doubleday, 1965). Hernton's major premise is that "the race problem is explicitly connected with sex" (4).

30. See Elshtain, Jean Bethke, *Women and War* (New York: Basic, 1987) 212–13; and Susan Schweik, "Writing War Poetry Like a Woman," *Critical Inquiry* 13 (1987) 532–56.

Notes to Chapter Three

1. Gwendolyn Brooks, *Annie Allen* (1949), rpt. in *Blacks* (Chicago: Third World P, 1987) 77–140.

2. Although Margaret Walker had received the Yale Series of Younger Poets Award in 1942 for her poems of social protest, *For My People* (New Haven: Yale UP, 1942), she would be unencumbered by the gauntlet of creating poetics amenable to a white audience; her next published work would be the historical novel, *Jubilee* (New York: Bantam, 1966).

3. A. P. Davis, "Integration and Race Literature," *Black Voices: An Anthology of Afro-American Literature*, ed. Abraham Chapman (New York: Mentor, 1968) 606–611. The essay was originally delivered at The First Conference of Negro Writers in March 1959 and published in *The American Negro Writer and His Roots* (New York: American Society of African Culture, 1960) 34–40. Davis is candid in his assertion that only "surface integration and token integration" exist for the Black writer: "we do not have actual integration anywhere" (607). However, he is optimistic that although these writers currently "will have to live between two worlds," the hope

for integration looms on the horizon because of the positive "spiritual climate" (607).

4. Alain Locke, "The New Negro," ed. *The New Negro: An Interpretation* (1925; New York: Arno, 1968).

5. The examples provided by Gloster of works with universal themes are Richard Wright, *Native Son* (New York: Harper, 1940); Willard Motley, *Knock on Any Door* (New York: D. Appleton–Century, 1947); Ann Petry, *The Street* (Boston: Beacon, 1946) and *A Country Place* (1947); Zora Neale Hurston, *Seraph On the Suwanee* (1948; New York: Harper, 1991); Gwendolyn Brooks, *Annie Allen* (New York: Harper, 1949); and the works of Frank Yerby.

6. Wright, *Native Son,* and Motley, *Knock On Any Door.* Ford also alludes to Frank Yerby, William Attaway, Ann Petry, Arna Bontemps, William Gardner Smith, and J. Saunders Redding, though he does not provide specific titles (374).

7. In a perceptive analysis, in contrast to Gloster, Ford targets several of the same authors to illustrate the inferiority of works that evade the racial orientation of the author. He sees Petry's *A Country Place* as "greatly inferior" because the author spent her energy "conjuring up vicarious experiences of a white society with which she was not minutely familiar"; Hurston's *Seraph* as "almost unbelievably inferior" to *Their Eyes Were Watching God* and *Mules And Men,* "her two novels of Negro life"; and Yerby's *The Golden Hawk* and *Pride's Castle,* "which completely ignore the racial angle," as inferior to the "greater artistic perfection" of his earlier two works, *The Foxes Of Harrow* and *The Vixens,* which both "have a background of Negro life and action" (375).

8. J. Saunders Redding, "American Negro Literature," *The American Scholar,* XVIII (1949):

137–148.

9. M. Walker, "New Poets," *Phylon* XI (1950): 345–354. Walker discusses how white critics seemed to "beg the question of the Negro's humanity, perhaps as an answer to the white patron's attitude that Negroes are only children anyway" (346). Arna Bontemps, "Negro Poets, Then and Now," *Phylon* XI (1950): 355–360. Bontemps articulates the feeling of "injustice" some poets felt when critics insistently labeled them "Negro poets": "As was the case with Countee Cullen, one gets the impression that Hayden is bothered by this Negro thing. He would like to be considered simply as a poet" (356–7).

10. Don L. Lee (Haki R. Madhubuti), "On *Kaleidoscope* and Robert Hayden," *Negro Digest* (Jan. 1968): 51–52, 90–94. Lee questions Hayden's editorship of a Negro Anthology given Hayden's resistance to being labeled a "Negro poet": "If one doesn't wish to be judged or recognized as a 'negro' poet, why advertise as such?" (51).

11. Hughes asserted his race consciousness by announcing that he was a "Black poet" and embarking upon a highly acclaimed career of writing vignettes about the ordinary folk of Harlem in *The Weary Blues* (1926) and *Fine Clothes To the Jew* (1927). The Jamaican poet Claude McKay nimbly negotiated the proving ground of using traditional poetic forms by making a remarkable alliance between the sonnet form and the wrath of his racial discontent with America, in poems like "America" and "If We Must Die." But the poet who was most at variance with his need for expression as a poet, without being confined to the characterizations of being a "Black poet," was Cullen. Educated at Harvard University, Cullen was at odds with the disparity he sensed between

racial identifications, his love of Keatsian verse, and his own fluidity in classical forms. He announced "I want to be known as a poet, not a Negro poet," to avoid the implied restriction of writing to racial themes and having his work judged solely on the merits of its expression of the Black struggle for equality. Though race consciousness is clear in the titles of his early works, *Color* (1925), *Copper Sun* (1927), *Ballad of a Brown Girl* (1928), and the anthology he edited, *Caroling Dusk* (1927), Cullen flinched at the idea of being labeled a "Negro poet," even in face of themes and imagery that often bespoke of his cultural heritage. See Jean Wagner, *Black Poets of the United States* (Urbana: U of Illinois P, 1973) for detailed information on the poets.

12. David Llorens, "Seeking a New Image: Writers Converge at Fisk University," *Negro Digest* (June 1966): 54–68. The conference was the site of Hayden's public disagreement with other Black writers over his stance (62). In Rosey E. Pool, *Beyond the Blues* (London: Hand and Flower, 1962), Hayden discusses when he wrote "propaganda rather than poetry" (24–25).

13. Llorens, *Negro Digest*, Tolson made his well-known comment at the same 1966 writer's conference attended by Hayden, n12.

14. Lee, *Kaleidoscope*, abruptly dismisses the technical proficiency of Tolson's work: "Melvin B. Tolson is represented with some of his less obscure poetry which still exhibits his range and his capacity to lose the people that may read him" (91). Paul Breman, "Poetry into the Sixties," *The Black American Writer*, Volume II: "poetry and drama", ed. C. W. E. Bigsby (Baltimore: Penguin, 1969) 99–109. Breman creates a trope from Shapiro's use of the word 'Negro' as a description for Tolson's language: ". . . Tolson postured for a white audience, and

with an ill–concealed grin and a wicked sense of humour gave it just what it wanted: an entertaining darkey using almost comically big words as the best WASP tradition demands of its educated house–niggers" (101).

Notes to Chapter Four

1. Suzanne Juhasz, *Naked and Fiery Forms: Modern American Poetry By Women* (New York: Octagon, 1976) 151.

2. Diane P. Freedman, *An Alchemy of Genres: Cross-Genre Writing by American Feminist Poet-Critics* (Charlottesville: U of Virginia P, 1992). Freedman discusses women's silence throughout, from the perspectives of a broad array of feminist poet–critics, but especially in "Discourse as Power" (1–25).

3. Brooke Kenton Horvath, "The Satisfactions of What's Difficult in Gwendolyn Brooks' Poetry," *American Literature* 62.4 (Dec. 1990): 606–616, offers an astute definition of a classic that is appropriate for the entire *Annie Allen* volume, though he applies it specifically to the poem "do not be afraid of no": it is "both timely and timeless, which is, after all, one definition of a classic" (616).

4. Melhem notes in *Heroic Voice* that "critical reaction to *Annie Allen* reflected the Harper editors' reception" (55). "The Anniad," originally titled "The Hesteriad," caused the most consternation among editors; even an outside reader, poet Genevieve Taggard, sensed a lack of cohesiveness in the work. As a result, editors mounted a campaign that culminated in Brooks making changes and omissions in the original manuscript. The proposed title of the book was changed from *Hester Allen* to *Annie Allen*, several poems from "The Womanhood" were omit-

ted; "Downtown Vaudeville" was altered; and the original poems "child's nightmare" and "food car in front of a mortuary" were replaced by new ones, "the rites for Cousin Vit" and "the parents: people like our marriage" (53). With a striking clarity of vision, reviewer Phyllis McGinley in "Poetry for Prose Readers," *New York Times Book Review* Jan. 1950: 7, perceives an unevenness in the work and comments: "The unevenness is, I hope very much, a fault of youth, and editors" (7).

5. Kate Daniels, "The Demise of the 'Delicate Prisons': The Women's Movement in Twentieth–Century American Poetry," *A Profile of Twentieth-Century American Poetry*, eds. Jack Myers and David Wojahn (Carbondale: Southern Illinois UP, 1991) 224–253. Daniels acknowledges Brooks' early achievements briefly: "Gwendolyn Brooks (born 1917) was the first American black woman poet to achieve national prominence and a significant critical reputation" (244). Like Ostriker, Daniels selects "the mother" as a poem that "addresses women." Brooks is also mentioned in Emily Stipes Watts, *The Poetry of American Women from 1632–1945* (Austin: U of Texas P, 1977) 7, 175.

6. A contrasting view is offered by Seibles, "A Quilt": "[Brooks'] was a poetry of deep intimacies, isolations, sensitive studies of individual interiors. . . The sensual swim of Brooks' diction and syntax, the secret sharing implied by it, marks the beginnings of a break from the more 'public' voices of the African American writers that preceded her" (174–75).

7. Adrienne Rich, "When We Dead Awaken: Writing as Re–Vision (1971)," *On Lies, Secretism and Silence: Selected Prose 1966–1978* (New York: Norton, 1979). Rich expands upon the idea of the woman–poet's "special" stature (38).

8. That Brooks fashioned a poetics "heard" and understood by Black women poet–critics is clear by the critical responses of writers like Hortense Spillers, Gladys Williams, Maria Mootry, and Claudia Tate, etc. See *A Life Distilled: Gwendolyn Brooks, Her Poetry and Fiction*, eds. Maria K. Mootry and Gary Smith (Urbana: U of Illinois P, 1987).

9. William Drake, "Poets as Mothers," *The First Wave: Women Poets in America 1915–1945* (New York: Macmillan, 1987). Drake's findings concur with the history of child–bearing as a source of "subtle but wrenching conflict for creative women. . . . her creative power was held to be either a substitute for motherhood or opposed to it, so that she was forced to confront a painful choice of priorities. . . . The majority of woman poets who rose to prominence between the World Wars did not, however, have children, indicating the choice of an artistic identity as opposed to the threat of anonymity that motherhood represented" (121–22). From a more personalized stance see Tillie Olsen, "Silences," in *Silences* (1965; New York: Delta/Seymour, 1979). By contrast, Brooks states: ". . . there was about a year—after the birth of my first child—when I scarcely put pen to paper; but except for that, I managed to keep at it" (*RPO* 178). Olsen states ". . . circumstances for sustained creation are almost impossible," given the interruptions and distractions of motherhood and its inherent responsibilities of "love, not duty" (33).

10. In Betsy Erkkila, *The Wicked Sisters: Women Poets, Literary History, and Discord* (New York: Oxford, 1992), Erkkila writes: "Rich has occasionally been singled out by black women as one of the few white feminists to insist on the need for white women to educate themselves about the experiences of black women and

the historical differences between black and white women" (181–82). Also see Rich, "Disloyal to Civilization: Feminism, Racism, Gynephobia" (*Lies* 275–310), and "Toward a More Feminist Criticism" and "Resisting Amnesia: History and Personal Life," *Blood, Bread, and Poetry: Selected Prose 1979–1985* (New York: Norton, 1986) 85–99, 136–59; Audre Lorde, "The Master's Tools Will Never Dismantle the Master's House," *Sister Outsider* (Trumansburg, New York: Crossing P, 1984), 113; Hortense Spillers, "Interstices: A Small Drama of Words," *Pleasure and Danger: Exploring Female Sexuality*, ed. Carole S. Vance (Boston: Routeledge & Kegan Paul, 1984) 81.

11. Erkkila, *Wicked*, constructs a framework from the presence of Black music forms "from the chants and hollers of the work field, to the gospels and spirituals of the church, to the blues and jazz performances of tent shows and cabarets" to explicate Brooks' work in an "African-American oral and folk culture" tradition (193).

12. Henry Louis Gates, foreword, *Collected Black Women's Poetry*, ed. Joan R. Sherman (New York: Oxford UP, 1988) vii–xxvi. Gates discusses the evolution of Black writers in a "matrilineal line of descent" since Phillis Wheatley launched both "the Black American literary tradition *and* the Black woman's literary tradition" with her 1773 publication. His concern, and the purpose of the collection is to recover previously inaccessible works by early Black women poets. Gates notes the irony that Wheatley's status of "progenitor of the black literary tradition" and the "important fact of common, coterminous literary origins seems to have escaped most scholars" (x). He situates that fact in the silence of the Black tradition of writing: "Black women writers dominated the final decade of the nineteenth century" (xii),

Renaissance—"racial assertion and poetic freedom,"—they were more inclined to write "personal" poetry and "aracial or quietly racial works in traditional forms" (174). Drake, *Wave,* also attests to the invisibility of Black women poets: "Black women poets in the 1920's occupied a position of far greater complexity, isolation, and difficulty than that of the white women poets with whom they shared no community whatever. . . . The Black women poets . . . not only published very little and attracted little attention but have remained in obscurity, victims of a particularly unsparing sexual oppression" (220).

15. Also see Gwendolyn Brooks, "Mothers and Daughters," *28 Land's End,* no. 5 (May 1992): 88; Gloria Joseph and Jill Lewis, "Black Mothers and Daughters: Their Roles and Functions in American Society," *Common Differences: Conflicts in Black and White Feminist Perspectives* (New York: Anchor, 1981) 75–126. Joyce Ladner, *Tomorrow's Tomorrow: The Black Woman* (New York: Doubleday/Anchor, 1971); Adrienne Rich, "Motherhood and Daughterhood," *Of Woman Born: Motherhood as Experience and Institution* (New York: Norton, 1976); "Mother's and Daughters I & II," *Sage: A Scholarly Journal on Black Women* 1 (Fall 1984) and 4 (Fall 1987).

16. Geneva Smitherman, *Talkin and Testifyin: The Language of Black America* (Detroit: Wayne State UP, 1977) defines "the African–derived communication process of call–response" by its use in ongoing interaction between the preacher and the congregation in sermonic patterns, "the singing style of black music," in the works of Black writers, and as "a basic organizing principle of Black American culture generally" (103–5).

17. Claudia Tate, "Anger So Flat: Gwendolyn Brooks'

but their writings "have remained buried in obscurity, accessible only in research libraries or in overpriced and poorly edited reprints" (xvi). Also, Joan R. Sherman, "Afro-American Women Poets of the Nineteenth Century: A Guide to Research and Bio-Bibliographies of the Poets," *All the Women Are White, All the Blacks Are Men, But Some of Us Are Brave,* eds. Gloria T. Hull, Patricia Bell-Scott, and Barbara Smith (New York: Feminist P, 1982) 245–260; Joan R. Sherman, *Invisible Poets: Afro-American Poets of the Nineteenth Century* (Urbana: U of Illinois P, 1974); Erlene Stetson, ed. *Black Sister: Poetry by Black Women 1746–1980* (Bloomington: U of Indiana P, 1981) represent the efforts of scholars to uncover the tradition of Black women's writings, especially poetry.

13. Brooks, *RPO,* discusses her many literary influences, especially Inez Stark 65–68 and 174; Hughes 70–71, 170, and 174; Countee Cullen 170; James Weldon Johnson 174. Gloria T. Hull, "Afro-American Women Poets: A Bio-Critical Survey," *Shakespeare's Sisters: Feminist Essays on Women Poets,* eds. Sandra M. Gilbert and Susan Gubar (Bloomington: Indiana UP, 1979) 165–182. Hull alludes to the stature of the male poets of the Harlem Renaissance and refers to McKay, Cullen, and Hughes as "the Big Three enshrined on a black Parnassus," while the women, Angelina Grimke, Anne Spencer, Georgia Douglas Johnson, Jessie Fauset, Effie Lee Newsome, Gwendolyn Bennett, and Helene Johnson served them "as handmaidens to the throne" (170).

14. Hull, "Poets," provides insight as to why the women poets of the Harlem Renaissance "are not better known or more highly rated." She explains that first "they did not publish and produce enough" and secondly, in contrast to the "prevailing concept" of the Harlem

Annie Allen," A Life Distilled: Gwendolyn Brooks, Her Poetry and Fiction, eds. Maria K. Mootry and Gary Smith (Urbana: U of Illinois P, 1987) 140–152. Tate interprets Annie's predilection for sleeping as a symbolic death that is symptomatic of her need to escape the rigors of confrontations with her mother and a foreshadowing of the repressed anger that will stifle her expression until she matures in "The Womanhood" (146).

18. Brooks, *RPO,* shares the written response of Johnson who read some of her poems: "You have an unquestionable talent and feeling for poetry. Continue to write—at the same time, study carefully the work of the best modern poets, not to imitate them, but to help cultivate the highest possible standard of self-criticism" (202); Stark instructed Brooks: "You must be careful not to list the obvious things" (*RPO* 66); and Richard Barksdale, "Trends in Contemporary Poetry, *Phylon* XIX (1958): 408–416, argues with Brooks' adaptation of the Modernist feature of compression and notes specifically that "The Anniad" is a story "stripped down to skeletal brevity" (413); Madhubuti, preface, *RPO,* who views Brooks' pre–1967 work as excessively cumbersome in technique, offers a contrasting view: "Gwendolyn Brooks' post–1967 poetry is fat–less. Her new work resembles a man getting off meat, turning to a vegetarian diet. What one notices immediately is that all the excess weight is quickly lost. Her work becomes extremely streamlined and to the point" (22).

19. Barksdale, "Poetry," affirms "the impressive example of modern poetical ellipsis" in *Annie Allen,* but also voices concern about the "numerous deletions" in "do not be afraid of no." He suggests that communication of the poem's content is "hampered when important nouns and verbs are so thoughtfully omitted. Miss

Brooks is undoubtedly inarticulate by design in these lines; but inarticulateness, whether artistically controlled or not, is still inarticulateness" (414).

20. Horvath, "Satisfactions," takes a passing glance at the interesting possibility that "do not be afraid of no" offers "a feminist commentary upon marriage" (611).

21. Melhem, *Heroic.* In contrast to Brooks' statement that she is not "form conscious" and that her stanza patterns is just a "Lucky seven . . . I imagine I finished one stanza, then decided that the rest of them would be just like that" (*RPO* 157–8), Melhem provides a minute analysis of rhyme royal versions in Brooks' septets and the early use of the ottava rima stanzaic form by Milton, Keats, and Byron to suggest similarities in "The Anniad" (62–3).

22. Toni Morrison, "Interview," *Newsweek* 30 (Mar. 1981): 52–57, states: "Art can be both uncompromisingly beautiful and socially responsible" (57).

23. David Littlejohn, "Negro Writers Today: The Poets," *Black On White: A Critical Survey of Writing By American Negroes* (New York: Grossman, 1966) protests extensive word play, allusion, and technique and suggests that she uses a "crisp Mandarin diction, ice-perfect sound to stand between the reader and the subject . . . [and] appears only to pretend to talk of things and of people; her real love is words" (90).

24. Stanley Fish, *Surprised By Sin: The Reader in Paradise Lost* (1967; Berkeley: U of California P, 1971), offers a fine analysis of reader-response criticism as he argues for the effectiveness of "authorial intrusion" in the epic voice of *Paradise Lost.*

25. Davis, "Black-and-Tan Motif"; these poems appear in *A Street in Bronzeville*; Hortense Spillers, "Gwendolyn the Terrible: Proposition on Eleven Poems,"

Distilled, offers astute commentary on how Brooks' use of the intraracial color struggle probes "the psychic and spiritual reaches of the black woman's soul. I know of no modern poet before Brooks to address this subject, and as she does so, she offers the female a way out not only by awakening the phobia, but also by regarding it as yet another style of absurdity" (228).

26. Walker, "Poets," writes: "Coming after the long hue and cry of white writers that Negroes as poets lack form and intellectual acumen, Miss Brooks' careful craftsmanship and sensitive understanding reflected in *Annie Allen* are not only personal triumphs but a racial vindication" (353).

27. Brooks, *RPO*, writes about her sonnet–ballad form: "Its one claim to fame is that I invented it" (186). Melhem, *Heroic*, writes of Brooks' invention: In "the moving coronach . . . the question–lament encircles the poems as it does Annie's life" (69).

28. Williams, "Brooks' Sonnet," notes Brooks' effectiveness in the use of metaphors that contribute to her economy with words and calls it a "metaphoric immediacy" in phrases like the "autumn freezing" of "What shall I give my children? who are poor" that depicts a societal shunning of the poor (232).

29. Williams, "Sonnet," writes that Brooks is "not successful" with her attempt to "integrate religious and bitter socio–political meanings in the same language," especially the "frugal vestibules" that convey the "cruelly neglectful attitude" of the dominant society toward the poor (233).

30. Williams, "Sonnet," takes an interesting look at Brooks' use of "sound, argument, and tone" to inform the children that fighting, not fiddling, is the vital lesson (235).

Notes to Chapter Five

1. Gwendolyn Brooks, *The Bean Eaters* (1960), rpt. in *Blacks* (Chicago: Third World P, 1987) 323–385.

2. Myrdal, *Dilemma*. See especially chapter 28, "The Basis of Social Inequality." Drake and Cayton, *Metropolis*, vol. 2. See especially chapter 14, "Bronzeville." Juan Williams, *Eyes On the Prize* (New York: Viking, 1987).

3. Langston Hughes, "Harlem," *Montage of a Dream Deferred*, (1951; New York: Vintage, 1974) 268. The poem opens with the line "What happens to a dream deferred?" directed at the urban residents of New York's Harlem community and is also applicable to the residents of Bronzeville who face the racial turbulence which is a precursor to the Civil Rights Movement of the 1960s.

4. Brooks, *RPO* (78).

5. In *Of Woman Born*, Rich recounts her own nurturing by a Black "mother." She writes: "As a child raised in what was essentially the South, Baltimore in the segregated 1930s, I had from birth not only a white, but a black mother. This relationship, so little explored, so unexpressed, still charges the relationships of black and white women" (253).

6. In *From Slavery to Freedom*, Franklin's study of lynching patterns yields the following synopsis: "Violent manifestations of hostility to blacks in the North and in the South were not new. They had persisted almost from the beginning of the Negro's presence in the New World . . . In the last sixteen years of the nineteenth century there had been more than 2,500 lynchings, the great majority of which were of Negroes, with

Mississippi, Alabama, Georgia, and Louisiana leading the nation . . . In the very first year of the new century more than 100 Negroes were lynched, and before the outbreak of World War I the number for the century had soared to more than 1,100. The South was far ahead of the rest of the country, but several Northern states, notably those in the Midwest, adhered to this ancient barbaric ritual of total disregard for the law. Although the impression was widely held that most of the Negroes lynched had been accused of raping white women, the records do not sustain this impression. In the first fourteen years of the twentieth century only 315 lynch victims were accused of rape or attempted rape, while more than 500 were accused of homicide and the others were accused of robbery, insulting white persons, and numerous other 'offenses.' Regardless of the alleged crime of the victim, lynching in the twentieth century continued to be an important, if illegal, part of the system of punishment in the United States" (282).

7. Where William Wells Brown used the subject of lynching as an aside in *Clotel* (1853; New York: Collier, 1980), as did Margaret Walker in *Jubilee* (New York: Bantam, 1967), lynching was central to the thematic structure of numerous works of literature. Some examples are Claude McKay's sonnet "The Lynching" (1922 *Harlem Shadows*; rpt. *Selected Poems of Claude McKay*, New York: Harcourt, 1953) 37, and several of Jean Toomer's selections such as the poem "Georgia Dusk," the narrative "Blood-Burning Moon," and the drama "Kabnis" in *Cane* (1923; New York: Liveright, 1975).

8. G. Malcolm Laws, *Native American Balladry* (Philadelphia: American Folklore Society, 1964) 85. In his study of balladry, Laws writes: "As in all balladry, there is a central event to be recounted. But the Negro

is not usually content merely to pass along the ballad as he heard it. In a sense he performs the ballad, sometimes adding comments between stanzas as well as incorporating in it details of interest which could apply to the incident being narrated, and which perhaps make it of more vital concern to the audience of the moment." Examples of improvisation in the ballad are most notable in the works of Sterling Brown, especially in his creation of the blues-ballad "Ma Rainey" (1932; *Southern Road;* rpt. *The Collected Poems of Sterling Brown*, selected by Michael S. Harper, New York: Harper, 1980) 62. Brown's ballad is hailed as a "literary phenomenon" by Stephen Henderson in *Understanding the New Black Poetry* (New York: Morrow, 1972) 51.

9. In a fictionalized version, Bebe Moore Campbell's *Your Blues Ain't Like Mine* (New York: Putman, 1992), creates a Southern setting that closely recalls the Emmett Till lynching. She too examines a lynching from the perspective of a white protagonist.

10. Extensive examinations of Southern race relations and their explicit sexual implications can be found in Calvin C. Hernton's *Sex and Racism in America* (New York: Doubleday, 1965) 16, Langston Hughes' "Home" in *The Ways of White Folk* (1933; New York: Vintage, 1990) 51–56, and Stephen Whitfield's *A Death in the Delta* (New York: Free P, 1988) 5.

11. Kent's inability to gain insight into Brooks' strategy of delving into the psychological maze of Carolyn Bryant's mind prevents his entrance into the larger realm of racism and sexism that intertwines to bind Bryant's psyche. In charging Brooks with rendering a false introspective account of Bryant's awakening, he attempts to dilute the use of gender as an issue to overcome odds heretofore insurmountable by race alone.

Interestingly, the poems which trouble Kent and "do not fulfill themselves" are primarily woman–centered poems such as: "the mother," "The Queen of the Blues," "The Ballad of Pearl Mae Lee" (*A Street in Bronzeville*), "A Bronzeville Mother Loiters in Mississippi. Meanwhile, a Mississippi Mother Burns Bacon," and "The Chicago *Defender* Sends a Man to Little Rock" (*The Bean Eaters*), as noted in Kent's *Blackness and the Adventure of Western Culture* (Chicago: Third World P, 1972) 120–121.

By contrast, in *Feminist Theory: From Margin to Center* (Boston: South End P, 1984), bell hooks provides an excellent theoretical perspective on why the "world view" of Black women differs considerably from that of Black men, white women, and white men. Since the marginality of Black women does not permit them to exploit or oppress others, they are endowed with a "special vantage point" from which to criticize the "racist, classist, sexist hegemony as well as create a counter hegemony" (15). Although Brooks does not overtly criticize the Southern patriarchal structure which holds Bryant hostage, she does reveal the world of silence in which Bryant exists and constructs a theoretical framework for a critical examination of racism and sexism.

12. Whitfield notes the "informal atmosphere" of the courtroom during the Till trial (38). In "Land of The Till Murder Revisited," *Ebony* (March 1986), Clotye Murdock Larsson writes: "The majority of the spectators at the Till trial were the White Mississippians. . . . With them they brought their children and their box lunches. They bought soft drinks from vendors who curtly refused to sell their wares to Blacks . . ." (56).

13. The somber portrayal of the Bronzeville mother is mindful of a stanza in Paul Laurence Dunbar's poem

"We Wear the Mask" from his *Lyrics of Lowly Life* (1899; rpt. *The Complete Poems of Paul Laurence Dunbar,* New York: Dodd, Mead, 1913) 219.

> Why should the world be overwise,
> In counting all our tears and sighs?
> Nay, let them only see us, while
> We wear the mask. (71)

14. Countee Cullen, "Christ Recrucified," *Kelly's* (1922; rpt. Jean Wagner, *Black Poets of the United States,* Urbana: U of Illinois P, 1973) 335. Symbolically, the figure of the crucified Christ is representative of the lynched black man as Cullen makes painfully clear in the final tercet of the sonnet:

> Christ's awful wrong is that he's black of hue,
> The sin for which no blamelessness atones;
> But lest the sameness of the cross should tire,
> They kill him now with famished tongues of fire,
> And while he burns, good men, and women, too,
> Shout, battling for his black and brittle bones. (13)

Works Cited

Angle, M. Paul. "We Asked Gwendolyn Brooks." Chicago: Illinois Bell Telephone, Summer 1967. Reprinted in *Report from Part One.* Detroit: Broadside, 1971. 131–146.

Review of *Annie Allen. Kirkus* 15 June 1949: 319.

—. *New Yorker* 17 Dec. 1949: 130.

Attaway, William. *Blood on the Forge.* 1941. New York: Collier Books, 1970.

—. *Let Me Breathe Thunder.* 1939. Chatham, N. J.: Chatham Bookseller, 1969.

Baker, Houston A., Jr. "The Achievement of Gwendolyn Brooks." *CLA* 1 (1972): 23–31.

Barksdale, Richard and Keneth Kinnamon, eds. *Black Writers of America.* New York: MacMillian, 1972.

Barksdale, Richard. "Trends in Contemporary Poetry." *Phylon* XIX (1958): 408–416.

Review of *The Bean Eaters. Booklist* 1 July 1960: 650.

—. *Bookmark.* Apr. 1960: 176.

—. *Virginia Kirkus* 1 Feb. 1960: 131.

Bell–Scott, Patricia, et al., eds. *Double Stitch: Black Women Write About Mothers and Daughters.* Boston: Beacon, 1991.

Bigsby, C. W. E. "The Black Poet as Cultural Sign." *The Second Black Renaissance: Essays in Black Literature.* Westport, CT: Greenwood Press, 1980.

Bock, Frederick. "A Prize Winning Poet Fails to Measure UP." *Chicago Tribune* 6 May 1960: 12.

Bone, Robert. "Richard Wright and the Chicago Renaissance." *Callaloo* 9.3 28 (1986): 446–468.

Bontemps, Arna. "Negro Poets, Then and Now." *Phylon* XI (1950): 355–360.

—. *Black Thunder.* 1936. Boston: Beacon, 1968.

Breman, Paul. "Poetry into the Sixties." *Poetry and Drama.* Vol. 2 *The Black American Writer. Ed.* C. W. E. Bigsby. Baltimore: Penguin, 1969.

Brooks, Gwendolyn. *Annie Allen.* New York: Harper & Brothers, 1949. Reprinted in *Blacks.* Chicago: Third World P, 1987.

—. *The Bean Eaters.* New York: Harper & Brothers, 1960. Reprinted in *Blacks.* Chicago: Third World P, 1987.

—. "GLR Interview: Gwendolyn Brooks." By Martha H. Brown. *Great Lakes Review* 60 (1979): 48–55.

—. Interview. *Black Women Writers.* Ed. Claudia Tate. New York: Continuum, 1984.

—. "Mothers and Daughters." *Land's End.* 5 May 1992: 88.

—. "Poets Who Are Negroes." *Phylon.* XI (1950): 312.

—. *Report From Part One.* Detroit: Broadside, 1972.

—. *Report From Part Two.* Chicago: Third World P, 1996.

—. *A Street in Bronzeville.* New York: Harper & Brothers, 1945. Reprinted in *Blacks.* Chicago: Third World P, 1987.

Brown, Frank London. *Trumbull Park.* Chicago: Regency, 1959.

Brown, Oscar Jr. "Elegy for a Plain Black Boy." Columbia. 1962.

Brown, Sterling. "Blues, Ballads, and Social Songs." *Seventy-five Years of Freedom.* Washington, D.C.: Library of Congress, 1940.

—. *Southern Road.* 1932 Reprinted in *The Collected Poems of Sterling A. Brown.* Selected by Michael S. Harper. New York: Harper, 1980.

Brown, William Wells. *Clotel.* 1853. New York: Collier, 1980.

Brownmiller, Susan. *Against Our Wills.* New York: Simon & Schuster, 1975.

Calloway, Earl. "Walter L. Lowe, Insurance Executive and the Last Mayor of Bronzeville, Dies." *Chicago Defender* 4 Aug. 1992: 3.

Campbell, Bebe Moore. *Your Blues Ain't Like Mine.* New York: Putman, 1992.

Christian, Barbara. "Afro–American Women Poets: A Historical Introduction." *Black Feminist Criticism: Perspectives on Black Women Writers*. New York: Pergamon, 1985.

Cullen, Countee. "Christ Recrucified." *Kelly's*. New York: Oct. 1922: 13. Reprinted in *Black Poets of the United States*. Jean Wagner. Urbana: U of Illinois P, 1973.

—. *Color*. New York: Harper, 1925.

—. *Copper Sun*. New York: Harper, 1927.

—, ed. *Caroling Dusk: An Anthology of Negro Poetry*. New York: Harper, 1927.

—. *Ballad of a Brown Girl*. New York: Harper, 1928.

Daniels, Kate. "The Demise of the 'Delicate Prisons': The Women's Movement in Twentieth–Century American Poetry." *A Profile of Twentieth-Century Poetry*. Eds. Jack Myers and David Wojahn. Carbondale: Southern Illinois UP, 1991.

Davis, Arthur P. "The Black–and–Tan Motif in the Poetry of Gwendolyn Brooks." *CLA* 6 Dec. 1962: 90–97.

—. "Integration and Race Literature." *The American Negro Writer and His Roots: Selected Papers From the First Conference of Negro Writers March 1959*. New York: American Society of African Culture, 1960. Reprinted in *Black Voices: An Anthology of Afro-American Literature*. Ed. Abraham Chapman. New York: Mentor, 1968.

Deutsch, Babette. "Six Poets." *Yale Review* 39 (1950): 361–5.

Drake, St. Clair and Horace Cayton. *Black Metropolis: A Study of Negro Life in a Northern City.* 2 vols. New York: Harper and Row, 1945; New York: Harcourt, 1962.

Drake, William. *The First Wave: Women Poets in America, 1915–1945.* New York: Macmillan, 1987.

Du Bois, W. E. B. *The Souls of Black Folk.* 1903. New York: Bantam, 1989.

Dunbar, Paul Laurence. "We Wear the Mask." 1899. *Lyrics of Lowly Life.* Reprinted in *The Complete Poems of Paul Laurence Dunbar.* New York: Dodd, Mead, 1913.

Ellison, Ralph. "Flying Home." *Cross Section.* Ed. Edwin Seaver. New York: L. B. Fisher, 1944.

—. *Invisible Man.* New York: Random, 1952.

—. "Richard Wright's Blues." *Shadow and Act.* New York: Signet, 1966.

Elshtain, Jean Bethke. *Women and War.* New York: Basic, 1987.

Erkkila, Betsy. *The Wicked Sisters: Women Poets, Literary History, and Discord.* New York: Oxford UP, 1992.

Fabre, Michel. *The Unfinished Quest of Richard Wright.* Trans. Isabel Barzun. New York: William Morrow, 1973.

Felgar, Robert. *Richard Wright.* Boston: Twayne, 1980.

Ferrill, Thomas Hornsby. Rev. of *Annie Allen*. *San Francisco Chronicle* 18 Sept. 1949: 18.

Fish, Stanley. *Surprised By Sin: The Reader in Paradise Lost*. 1967. Berkeley: U of California P, 1971.

Flug, Michael. "Harsh, Vivian Gordon (1890–1960)." *Black Women in America: An Historical Encyclopedia*. 2 vols. Ed. Darlene Clark Hine. Bloomington: Indiana UP, 1993.

Ford, Nick Aaron. "A Blueprint for Negro Authors." *Phylon* XIX (1958): 374–376.

Franklin, John Hope and Alfred A. Moss, Jr. 1947. *From Slavery to Freedom*. New York: Knopf, 1988.

Frazier, E. Franklin. *The Negro Family in Chicago*. Chicago: U of Chicago P, 1932.

Freedman, Diane. *An Alchemy of Genres: Cross-Genre Writing by American Feminist Poet-Critics*. Charlottesville: U of Virginia P, 1992.

Gates, Henry Louis, Jr. Foreword. *Collected Black Women's Poetry*. Ed. Joan R. Sherman. New York: Oxford UP, 1988.

Giovanni, Nikki. *Black Judgement*. New York: Afro Arts, 1969.

Glauber, Rohert H. "Our Miss Brooks: Lyricist." Rev. of *Selected Poems*. *Chicago Sun-Times* 22 Sept. 1963: 1–2.

Gloster, Hugh M. "Race and the Negro Writer." *Phylon* XI (1950): 369–371.

Harris, Trudier. *Exorcising Blackness: Historical and Literary Lynching and Burning Rituals.* Bloomington: Indiana UP, 1984.

Hayden, Robert. "A Ballad of Remembrance." *Selected Poems.* New York: October House, 1966.

—. *Heart-Shape in the Dust.* Detroit: Falcon, 1940.

—. *The Lion and the Archer.* N. p., 1948.

—, ed. *Kaleidoscope: Poems by Negro Poets.* New York: Harcourt, 1967.

Henderson, Stephen. *Understanding the New Black Poetry.* New York: Morrow, 1972.

Hernton, Calvin C. *Sexism and Racism in America.* New York: Doubleday, 1965.

Himes, Chester. *If He Hollers Let Him Go.* New York: Signet, 1945.

hooks, bell (Gloria Watkins). *Feminist Theory: From Margin to Center.* Boston: South End, 1984.

Horvath, Brooks Kenton. "The Satisfactions of What's Difficult in Gwendolyn Brooks' Poetry." *American Literature* 62 (Dec. 4, 1990): 606–616.

Hughes, Langston. "The Negro Artist and the Racial Mountain." *Nation* 122 (June 23, 1926): 692–94.

—. "When Sue Wears Red." *The Dreamkeeper.* 1937. Reprinted in *Selected Poems.* New York: Vintage, 1974.

—. "Harlem." *Montage of a Dream Deferred.* 1951. Reprinted in *Selected Poems.* New York: Vintage, 1974.

—. *The Best of Simple.* New York: Hill and Wang, 1961.

Huie, William Bradford. "The Shocking Story of Approved Killing in Mississippi." *Look* 24 Jan. 1956: 46–48.

Humphries, Rolfe. "Bronzeville." *New York Times Book Review* 4 Nov. 1945.

Hurston, Zora Neale. *Seraph on the Suwanee.* 1948. New York: Harper, 1991.

—. *Their Eyes Were Watching God.* 1937. Urbana: U of Illinois P, 1980.

Jemie, Onwuchekwa. "Hughes and the Evolution of Consciousness in Black Poetry." *Langston Hughes: An Introduction to Poetry.* New York: Columbia UP, 1975. 167–171.

Johnson, James Weldon and Rosamond Johnson. "O Black and Unknown Bards." Preface. *The Books of American Negro Spirituals.* Reprint. New York: Viking, 1953. 11.

Jones, Hettie. *Big Star Fallin' Mama: Five Women in Black Music.* New York: Dell, 1974.

Joseph, Gloria and Jill Lewis. *Common Differences: Conflicts in Black and White Feminist Perspectives.* New York: Norton,

1976.

Juhasz, Suzanne. *Naked and Fiery Forms: Modern American Poetry by Women*. New York: Octagon, 1976.

Keats, John. "La Belle Dame sans Merci." *The Norton Anthology of Poetry*. Ed. Arthur M. Eastman. New York: Norton, 1970. 693.

Kennedy, Leo. "Chicago's Finest Writer." *Chicago Sun-Times* 29 Aug. 1949: 43.

Kent, George. *Blackness and the Adventure of Western Culture*. Chicago: Third World P, 1972. 104–138.

—. *A Life of Gwendolyn Brooks*. Lexington, Ky: U of Kentucky P, 1990.

Kinnamon, Keneth. "Call and Response: Intertextuality in Two Autobiographical Works by Richard Wright and Maya Angelou." *Studies in Black American Literature: Belief vs. Theory in Black American Literary Criticism*. Joe Weixlmann and Chester J. Fontenot, eds. Greenwood, Florida: Penkevill, 1986.

Kunitz, Stanley. "Bronze By Gold." *Poetry* LXXVI (1950): 53–56.

Ladner, Joyce. *Tomorrow's Tomorrow: The Black Woman*. New York: Anchor, 1972.

Laws, G. Malcolm. *Native American Balladry*. Philadelphia: American Folklore Society, 1964.

Lewis, Ida. "Conversations: Gwen Brooks and Ida Lewis: 'My People are Black People'" *Essence* April 1971. Reprinted in

Gwendolyn Brooks, *Report From Part One.* Detroit: Broadside, 1971.

Lincoln, C. Eric and Lawrence H. Mamiya. *The Black Church in the African American Experience.* Durham: Duke UP, 1990.

Littlejohn, David. "Negro Writers Today: The Poets." *Black on White: Critical Survey of Writing by American Negroes.* New York: Grossman, 1966.

Llorens, David. "Seeking a New Image: Writers Converge at Fisk University." *Negro Digest* June 1966: 54–68.

Locke, Alain. "The New Negro." Ed. *The New Negro: An Interpretation.* 1925. New York: Arno, 1969.

Lorde, Audre. "Audre Lorde." *Black Women Writers at Work.* Ed. Claudia Tate. New York: Continuum. 1984.

—. *Sister Outsider.* Trumansburg, New York: Crossing, 1984.

Madhubuti, Haki (Don L. Lee). "On *Kaleidoscope* and Robert Hayden." *Negro Digest* Jan. 1968: 51–2, 90–4.

—. Preface. *Report From Part One.* Detroit: Broadside, 1972. 13–30.

—, ed. *Say That the River Turns: The Impact of Gwendolyn Brooks.* Chicago: Third World, 1987.

McDougald, Elise Johnson. "The Task of Negro Womanhood." *The New Negro: An Interpretation.* Ed. Alain Locke. 1925. New York: Arno, 1968.

McGinley, Phyllis. "Poetry For Prose Readers." *New York Times Book Review* 22 Jan. 1950: 7.

McKay, Claude. *Harlem Shadows.* 1922. Reprinted in *Selected Poems of Claude McKay.* New York: Harcourt, 1953.

Melhem, D. H. *Gwendolyn Brooks: Poetry and the Heroic Voice.* Kentucky: U of Kentucky P, 1987.

Miller, R. Baxter. "'Does Man Love Art?': The Humanistic Aesthetic of Gwendolyn Brooks." Ed. *Black American Literature and Humanism.* Kentucky: U of Kentucky P, 1981.

"Mississippi Barbarism." *Crisis* 62 (Oct. 1955): 480–81.

Mootry, Maria K. and Gary Smith, eds. *A Life Distilled: Gwendolyn Brooks, Her Poetry and Fiction.* Urbana: U of Illinois P, 1987.

Motley, Willard. *Knock on Any Door.* New York: D. Appleton–Century, 1947.

Mphahlele, Ezekiel. *Voices in the Whirlwind.* New York: Hill and Wang, 1967.

Mullen, Robert W. *Blacks in America's Wars: The Shift in Attitudes from the Revolutionary War to Vietnam.* New York: Pathfinder, 1974.

Myrdal, Gunnar. *The American Dilemma.* New York: Harper, 1944.

"Nation Horrified By Murder of Kidnaped Chicago Youth." *Jet* 15 Sept. 1955. Reprinted in *Jet* 12 Aug. 1991.

Naylor, Gloria. *The Women of Brewster Place.* New York: Penguin, 1983.

Olsen, Tillie. *Silences.* 1965. New York: Delta/Seymour, 1979.

Ostriker, Alicia Suskin. *Stealing the Language: The Emergence of Women's Poetry in America.* Boston: Beacon, 1986.

Petry, Ann. *The Street.* 1946. Boston: Beacon, 1974

—. *A Country Place.* Boston: Beacon, 1947.

Pool, Rosey E., ed. *Beyond the Blues: New Poems by American Negroes.* England: Hand and Flower, 1962.

Redding, J. Saunders. "Cellini-like Lyrics." *Saturday Evening Review* 17 Sept. 1949: 23, 27.

—. "Race and the Negro Writer." *Phylon* XI (1950): 369–373.

—. "American Negro Literature." *The American Scholar* XVIII (1959): 137–148.

Redmond, Eugene B. "A Long Way From Home." *Drumvoices: A Critical History.* New York: Anchor, 1976.

Rich, Adrienne. *Blood, Bread, and Poetry: Selected Prose 1979–1985.* New York: Norton, 1986.

—. *Of Woman Born.* New York: Norton, 1976.

—. "When We Dead Awaken: Writing as Re–Vision (1971)." *On Lies, Secrets, and Silences: Selected Prose 1966–1978.* New York: Norton, 1976.

Robinson, Theresa Jontyle and Wendy Greenhouse. *The Art of Archibald J. Motley, Jr.* Chicago: Chicago Historical Society, 1991.

Russell, Kathy, Midge Wilson, and Ronald Hall. *The Color Complex: The Politics of Skin Color among African Americans.* New York: Harcourt, 1992.

Sadler, Lew. "Say Dixie Whites Are Not Bad Folk." *Chicago Defender* 24 Sept. 1955: 7. Reprinted in Juan Williams, *Eyes on the Prize.* New York: Viking, 1987. 55.

Salter, Mary Jo. "A Poem of One's Own." *The New Republic* 4 March 1991: 30–34.

Scheweik, Susan. "Writing War Poetry Like a Woman." *Critical Inquiry* 13 (1987): 532–56.

Seibles, Timothy. "A Quilt in Shades of Black: The Black Aesthetic in Twentieth–Century African American Poetry." *A Profile of Twentieth-Century American Poetry.* Eds. Jack Myers and David Wojahn. Carbondale: Southern Illinois UP, 1991. 159–189.

Shapiro, Harvey. "A Quartet of Younger Singers." *New York Times Book Review* 23 Oct. 1960: 32.

Shaw, Harry B. "Perceptions of Men by Gwendolyn Brooks." *Black American Poets Between Worlds.* Ed. R. Baxter Miller. Knoxville: U of Tennessee P, 1986. 136–159.

Sherman, Joan R. “Afro–American Women Poets of the Nineteenth Century: A Guide Research and Bio–Bibliographies of the Poets.” *All the Women Are White, All the Blacks Are Men, But Some of Us Are Brave.* Eds. Gloria T. Hull, Patricia Bell–Scott, and Barbara Smith. New York: Feminist Press, 1982.

—. *Invisible Poets: Afro-American Poets of the Nineteenth Century.* Urbana: U of Illinois P, 1974.

Smith, Gary. “Brooks' ‘We Real Cool.’” *The Explicator* 43–2 Winter 1985: 49–50.

Smitherman, Geneva. *Talkin and Testifyin: The Language of Black America.* Detroit: Wayne State U P, 1977.

Spillers, Hortense J. “Gwendolyn the Terrible: Proposition on Eleven Poems.” *A Life Distilled: Gwendolyn Brooks, Her Poetry and Fiction.* Eds. Maria K. Mootry and Gary Smith. Urbana: U of Illinois P, 1987. 224–238.

—. “Interstices: A Small Drama of Words.” *Pleasure and Danger: Exploring Female Sexuality.* Ed. Carole S. Vance. Boston: Routledge & Kegan Paul, 1984. 73–99.

Stanford, Ann Folwell. “Dialectics of Desire: War and the Restive Voice in Gwendolyn Brooks' ‘Negro Hero’ and ‘Gay Chaps at the Bar.’” *African American Review* 26 (1992): 197–211.

Stavros, George. “An Interview with Gwendolyn Brooks.” *Report Form Part One.* Detroit: Broadside, 1972. 147–166.

Stetson, Erlene, ed. *Black Sister: Poetry by Black Women 1746–1980.* Bloomington: U of Indiana P, 1981.

Review of *A Street in Bronzeville. Kirkus.* 15 July 1945: 306.

—. *New Yorker* 22 Sept. 1945: 80.

Strouse, Jean. "Toni Morrison's Black Magic." *Newsweek* 30 Mar. 1981: 52–57.

Tate, Claudia. "Anger So Flat: Gwendolyn Brooks' *Annie Allen.*" *A Life Distilled: Gwendolyn Brooks, Her Poetry and Fiction.* Eds. Maria. K Mootry and Gary Smith. Urbana: U of Illinois P, 1987. 140–152.

—, ed. *Black Women Writers at Work.* New York: Continuum, 1984.

Tolson, Melvin B. *Libretto for the Republic of Liberia.* New York: Twayne, 1953.

—. *Rendezvous with America.* New York: Dodd, Mead, 1944.

Toomer, Jean. *Cane.* 1923. New York: Liveright, 1975.

Travis, Dempsey. *Autobiography of Black Chicago.* Chicago: Urban Research Institute, 1981.

Wagner, Jean. *Black Poets of the United States.* Trans. Kenneth Douglas. Urbana: U of Illinois P, 1973.

Walker, Alice. "Letter to Editor." *New York Times Review* 30 Nov. 1975: 65–66.

Walker, Margaret. *For My People.* New Haven: Yale UP, 1942.

—. *Jubilee.* 1966. New York: Bantam, 1967.

—. "New Poets." *Phylon* XI (1950): 345–360.

Watts, Emily Stipes. *The Poetry of American Women from 1632–1945.* Austin: U of Texas P, 1977.

Webb, Constance. *Richard Wright: A Biography.* New York: Putnam, 1968.

Werner, Craig. "Leon Forrest and the AACM and the Legacy of the Chicago Renaissance." *Black Scholar* 23.3–4 (1993): 10–23.

Whitfield, Stephen. *A Death in the Delta: The Story of Emmett Till.* New York: Free P, 1988.

Wilder, Amos N. "Sketches from Life." *Poetry* III (1950): 164–6.

Williams, Gladys. "The Ballads of Gwendolyn Brooks." *A Life Distilled: Gwendolyn Brooks, Her Poetry and Fiction.* Eds. Maria K. Mootry and Gary Smith. Urbana: U of Illinois P, 1987. 205–223.

—. "Gwendolyn Brooks' Way With the Sonnet." *CLA* 2 (1968): 215–240.

Williams, Juan. *Eyes On the Prize.* New York: Viking, 1987.

Wright, Richard. "Introduction: Blueprint for Negro Writing." *New Challenge* II (1937): 53–65. Reprinted in *The Black Aesthetic.* Ed. Addison Gayle, Jr. New York: Doubleday, 1971. 315–326.

—. *Uncle Tom's Children.* 1940. New York: Harper; New York: Perennial, 1965.

—. *Native Son.* 1940. New York: Harper; New York: Perennial, 1966.

—. *Lawd Today.* New York: Avon, 1963.

Yerby, Frank. *The Foxes of Harrow.* New York: Dial, 1946.

—. *The Golden Hawk.* New York: Dial, 1948.

—. *Pride's Castle.* New York: Dial, 1949.

—. *The Vixens.* New York: Dial, 1947.

INDEX

L

Q

R